PERFECT PERIL

PERFECT PERIL:
Christian Science and Mind Control

Linda S. Kramer, Ph.D.

All Scripture quotes are taken from the KJV Bible, unless otherwise stated.

ISBN: 1503003930
ISBN 13: 9781503003934

For Jack

Acknowledgments

Many people have assisted me throughout the journey that resulted in this book. You know who you are—friends, counselors, pastors, family members, and colleagues. I thank you for your love, for your guidance, and for helping me through the tough times. God bless you all.

Contents

Author's Note, 2010

This book was first printed under the publisher-imposed title, *The Religion that Kills – Christian Science: Abuse, Neglect, and Mind Control.* I strongly objected to this harsh, sensational title because it was out of character with the book's "direct but fair" tone and made the book emotionally inaccessible to some of the people it was written to help. Eleven years later my publisher is long out of business—perhaps, in part, because of poor book-titling skills—and I am free to change the title to something more appropriate. I have chosen, *Perfect Peril: Christian Science and Mind Control.* While teaching its followers that they are spiritually perfect, Christian Science lures them into physical, emotional, and spiritual peril.

When I wrote this book in the late 1990's, the Christian Science Church was involved in an aggressive, multi-faceted marketing program designed to mainstream itself and attract new members. That program was unsuccessful and the Church continues to shrink. Nevertheless, the need for my message continues. Those who remain in Christian Science are still in peril, and many former Christian Scientists are still searching for emotional and spiritual freedom.

Perfect Peril remains largely as originally published except for minor wording changes, updates to the Resources section, some minor chapter rearrangement and, of course, the title.

Introduction

I grew up in Christian Science, never dreaming that I would one day leave it, much less write a book critical of it. I left the religion for doctrinal reasons but found that, somehow, I remained its emotional prisoner. I was out of Christian Science, but it was definitely not out of me. My long search for emotional freedom led me into the study of mind control. Through much research, many conversations, and a tremendous amount of introspection, I discovered a striking similarity between my emotional issues and those suffered not only by many former Christian Scientists, but also by the former members of several different cults. I reluctantly had to acknowledge that, despite its many good points, Christian Science involves mind control and can be quite emotionally damaging.

I have talked with many former Christian Scientists who cannot understand their deep insecurities and relentless emotional struggles. Upon hearing or reading about my recovery process, many have been amazed by how closely my experiences and conclusions mesh with their own. Several former Christian Scientists have commented that my words have finally given them a way to describe years of undefined pain.

Having discovered that my insights are genuinely helping people, and at the urging of many who have heard my story, I decided that it might be prudent to put my thoughts into book form. Little did I know how fascinating, enlightening, time-consuming, intellectually challenging, and painful this project would be. My goal was not to construct a wholly negative image of Christian Science, but to clearly identify the logic behind how this religion of perfection and love can create such havoc in the lives of its members. I wanted to let the Christian Scientists speak for themselves, so I spent months poring through thousands of pages of pro-Christian Science material and really getting to know Mrs. Eddy and her most ardent supporters. These people came alive to me through their writings, and I found myself respecting their devotion and caring for them as individuals. I also grieved as I watched them become ensnared in some dangerous thinking patterns.

My research took me through periods of amazement, amusement, grief, anger, exhaustion, enlightenment, and fear (it's not easy to discuss the shortcomings of a group I truly loved and trusted for thirty years). Writing the book has brought great emotional resolution. I have found that I can fully recognize the shortcomings of my former religion while still appreciating the good that it brought into my life. I am like an immigrant from a troubled country; I am happy and fulfilled in my new life, but some of my roots and affections will always remain with my homeland and its people.

This book is a labor of love, both for those who wish to understand the stark realities of Christian Science and for those who are trying to recover from them. In this book, I allow the Christian Scientists to do much of the talking, as I want them to be the ones who clarify both the attraction and the pitfalls of their religion. Readers unfamiliar with Christian Science may find the quotes perplexing and cumbersome as they encounter Mrs. Eddy's writing style and interesting use of capital letters. My advice to these readers is to simply treat the quotes as documentation, and avoid becoming bogged down in trying to understand the logic of each excerpt.

Chapters 1-12 evaluate Christian Science from a secular, psychological standpoint. "My Story—A Journey to Freedom" then tells my story of loving, leaving, and recovering from Christian Science. Finally, "Christian Science and the Bible" compares Christian Science to the Bible on several key doctrinal issues, points out how easily the practice of Christianity can become unbalanced, and offers my own opinion that biblical Christianity is really very simple. By separating the book's secular and religious discussions, I have attempted to make it emotionally accessible to a variety of readers. Nevertheless, I hope that each reader will explore the entire book. Only then can he or she fully understand Christian Science and its challenges.

CHAPTER ONE
Something is Wrong

A Perfect Discovery

Christian Science was "discovered" by Mary Baker Eddy in 1866. According to Church history, she slipped on a patch of ice and was severely injured. She was expected to die but turned to her Bible and was healed. As she earnestly studied the Bible during the next few years, God revealed to her the scientific system of healing that she named Christian Science. In 1875, Mrs. Eddy published her revelation in a book called *Science and Health.* She spent the next three decades revising her book, training converts, and founding a new religion based upon her revelation and teachings. By the time she died in 1910, she was the leader of a religious empire with approximately a hundred thousand members.

In Mrs. Eddy's day, Christian Science had much to offer a culture in which medicine was primitive and mind cures were a popular alternative. It also provided exciting ideas for a society that enjoyed exploring new philosophies. Christian Science taught that God's creation, including man, was entirely spiritual and good. All evil, including sickness and death, was an illusion which could be overcome by understanding one's true identity as a perfect, spiritual reflection of God. This "spiritual understanding" offered victory over life's problems—illness, poverty, and anything else that did not fit into a perfect worldview.

Christian Science also offered freedom from eternal judgment. If evil is unreal then hell does not exist—and there is no need for redemption as described by traditional Christianity. In fact, the premise that evil and matter are unreal demands that nearly every traditional Christian doctrine be given a "spiritualized" meaning in order to conform to the paradigm that all is spiritual and good. Thus, Christian Science differs from traditional Christianity in nearly every central doctrine—in its concept of God, of Jesus' identity and mission, of judgment and salvation, and of the Trinity—to name a few.

Mrs. Eddy and her followers believed that she was the divinely chosen Revelator to this age. They also believed that God gave her specific instructions on how to run her church. She wrote *The Manual of the Mother Church,* a "divinely inspired" set of by-laws for the central church, The First Church of Christ, Scientist, in Boston (also called The Mother Church). *The Manual* is designed specifically for The Mother Church, but its influence reaches directly into the teachings and functions of all Christian Science "branch" churches. Because they were divinely inspired, these by-laws and policies cannot be changed. A hundred years after her death, Mrs. Eddy still exercises great influence over the church she founded.

I said above that Christian Science offered (and still offers) much to its adherents— knowledge of their spiritual perfection, a spiritually scientific method of healing, and a new and very positive religious doctrine. But the sad truth is that Christian Science operates from a flawed premise. Matter *is* real and bad things *do* happen. While it delivers much that is good (like sound moral values), Mrs. Eddy's religion falls short of its utopian promises. In doing so, it often causes much suffering and emotional damage among its followers. The extent and tragedy of this damage will become apparent in the pages that follow.

Troubling Questions and the Search for Answers

Many of us who have left Christian Science find ourselves struggling with troubling questions. While involved with the religion we faced life with a positive attitude and a conquering spirit. We thought that we had Ultimate Truth and the means with which to solve life's problems. We thought that we were free.

Now that we are out of Christian Science we are left with the nagging feeling that something was terribly wrong. We look back and realize that, although our experience provided many good memories and offered us solid moral values, we carry emotional and physical scars suggesting that we were not so free after all. We remember unexplained deaths and feeling guilty when we were sick. We also remember the constant struggle between what our physical senses told us and how we were supposed to interpret them.

Most of us grew up in Christian Science and had no reference points against which to evaluate our feelings and religious culture. Whether or not we felt loved by our parents, most of us remember suffering needlessly with treatable diseases. Some of us recall being punished or neglected during times of illness (my parents did not punish or neglect me). We tolerated much more pain than is necessary in this modern age, even as we thought we were overcoming the false belief that sin, disease, and death are real.

As I recall my 30 years in Christian Science I find myself asking, "Why did I see (and ignore) so much quiet suffering? Why have I observed and heard of so many emotional difficulties among the grown children of 'good, strong' Christian Science families? How can Christian Scientists be so loving and full of good intentions, and yet have so much trouble truly empathizing with the needs of others?" As I ponder these and other questions, I am left with the feeling that Christian Scientists are denied their fundamental right to be human and to acknowledge the natural instincts that go along with their humanness. They live in a dual reality which allows them to be loving yet insensitive and to participate in the material world even while denying its existence. They live in what I call the "perfect bondage," a belief system that promises health, success, and spiritual perfection *as long as* they remain safely within the confines of Christian Science doctrine. To abandon the doctrine is to open oneself up to the illusory, but lethal, powers of "mortal mind."

Is Christian Science a cult? Are its followers the victims of mind control? In a word, yes—but please read on and allow me to explain my conclusions. If the terms "cult" and "mind control" offend you, let me assure you that they bother me too. I was a Christian Scientist and member of The Mother Church for a long time. I carried a strong emotional attachment to the religion and its leader for many years after leaving its ranks for doctrinal reasons. Nevertheless, I have faced the truth about my old beliefs and feel compelled to share what I have learned.

This book is the result of a long and sincere search for truth and emotional resolution. It is not intended to hurt anyone or to extol a particular religious denomination, but simply to help explain what happened to me and to many others I have met. While it should prove informative to anyone interested in learning about Christian Science "from the inside out," it is written primarily for three audiences. First, it is written for those who have lived Christian Science and are now suffering emotional fallout from the experience. Second, the book is written for those who want to understand how Christian Scientists think and why they suffer needlessly from easily treatable diseases. Finally, it is written for those who want to discuss biblical issues with former or current Christian Scientists, but who first need to scale the language barrier that Mary Baker Eddy so elegantly constructed around her followers.

My general approach will be to compare Christian Science to a widely accepted model for mind control and determine the commonalities between the two. The comparison will require some background information including the following:

- A brief overview of Christian Science doctrine
- A description of my source materials, most of which are pro-Christian Science
- A discussion of Mrs. Eddy's background, personality, leadership style, and alleged role in biblical prophecy
- A description of basic mind control theory

We will examine Christian Science in light of the mind control model, both as this religion was practiced in Mrs. Eddy's time and as it is practiced today. Our investigation will rely heavily on Mrs. Eddy's writings, on comments by her followers, and on case histories.

One of the driving forces behind this endeavor is the need to publicly address two questions. First, what is it about this religion that makes people subject themselves and their children to needless suffering and sometimes death? Second, why do so many people consider Christian Science to be just another benign religion, failing to notice the destruction it often leaves in its path?

CHAPTER TWO
Christian Science Doctrine

Christian Science is heavily based on the first chapter of Genesis. Its foundation can be summarized by two Bible verses:

> So God created man in his *own* image, in the image of God created he him; male and female created he them. (Gen. 1:27).

> And God saw every thing that he had made, and, behold, *it was* very good (Gen. 1:31a).

As defined by Christian Science, God is not a Personality but is better represented by a set of qualities and definitions. The glossary in *Science and Health* defines God as:

> The great I AM; the all-knowing, all-seeing, all-acting, all-wise, all-loving, and eternal; Principle; Mind; Soul; Spirit; Life; Truth; Love; all substance; intelligence.[1]

Mrs. Eddy concluded that since God is spiritual and made everything good, all that He created must also be spiritual and good. If God and His creation are spiritual and perfect, it follows that there can be no matter and no sin, sickness, or death. Mrs. Eddy defines matter as:

> Mythology; mortality; another name for mortal mind;[2] illusion; . . . the opposite of God; that of which immortal Mind takes no cognizance; that which mortal mind sees, feels, hears, tastes, and smells only in belief.[3]

The "Scientific Statement of Being," read every week from every Christian Science pulpit, begins with "There is no life, truth, intelligence, nor substance in matter" and ends with "Therefore man is not material; he is spiritual."[4]

A Christian Scientist's goal is to fully understand his spiritual nature and the unreality of matter. As he grows in his understanding of these truths as defined by Christian Science, his experience begins to reflect this understanding in the form of healings and in the overcoming of life's challenges. A healing is often called a "demonstration" because it shows, or demonstrates, the unreality of matter and the spiritual nature of God's creation. Christian Science never really explains where mortal mind came from or why it seems to exist—it just does (seemingly), and it must be challenged at every turn as it constantly tries to convince us that what we feel, hear, smell, taste, see, and touch are real.

Christian Scientists differentiate between Christian Science healing and the mere "faith healing" experienced in other denominations and sometimes by misguided Christian Scientists. Mrs. Eddy made this distinction quite clear in an article she wrote in September of 1910. The article states, in part,

> The sick, like drowning men, catch at whatever drifts toward them. The sick are told by a faith-Scientist, "I can heal you, for God is all, and you are well, since God creates neither sin, sickness, nor death." Such statements result in the sick either being healed by their faith in what you tell them—which heals only as a drug would heal, through belief—or in no effect

whatever. If the faith healer succeeds in *securing* (kindling) the belief of the patient in his own recovery, the practitioner will have performed a faith-cure which he mistakenly pronounces Christian Science. . . . Christian Science is not a faith-cure, and unless human faith be distinguished from scientific healing, Christian Science will again be lost from the practice of religion as it was soon after the period of our great Master's scientific teaching and practice.[5]

The point is that Mrs. Eddy defined Christian Science as a scientific system of healing, based upon specific spiritual laws she claimed were revealed to her straight from God. One must follow Mrs. Eddy's teachings without addition or deviation if he or she wishes to practice true Christian Science with consistent success. Mrs. Eddy is the revealer to this age, as Jesus was in His day, and she must be obeyed as such.[6]

A Christian Science healing does not consist of knowing that, for instance, a burned hand is not really burned. Trying to heal the burn would be admitting that there is a material hand to be burned in the first place. As Mrs. Eddy states in *Science and Health,*

Admit the existence of matter, and you admit that mortality (and therefore disease) has a foundation in fact. Deny the existence of matter, and you can destroy the belief in material conditions.[7]

A Christian Science healing involves understanding that as the perfect, spiritual reflection of God, one does not have a physical hand to be burned. As the Christian Scientist claims and understands that his true identity is purely spiritual, this understanding is reflected in his experience, and the burn is no longer manifested on his body (i.e., he is healed).

In Christian Science, the importance of understanding man's spiritual identity is illustrated by a conversation Mrs. Eddy held with several of her key workers. According to Annie Knott, Mrs. Eddy read the following words that she found in a *Christian Science Sentinel* article published 30

September 1905: "a diseased body is not acceptable to God." After quizzing the workers as to the accuracy of the statement she asked the question, "Now, will you, any of you tell me whether God has any more use for a well body than for a sick one?" Annie Knott continues, "This came like a flash of light, and we all wondered at our own dullness."[8]

The vast misconception that we and the world around us are material is summed up by the term "mortal mind." We live, receive pleasure, and suffer from the seeming laws of mortal mind as long as we believe that they are true. Sooner or later we must all learn that mortal mind is an illusion. We suffer from its apparent effects until we learn the lesson. Death does not excuse us from learning the lesson, but simply represents a phase through which we pass as we continue to believe in our mortality. We will suffer on the next "plane(s) of existence" (i.e., state[s] of consciousness) until we learn that we are sinless, spiritual ideas of God (this is not considered to be reincarnation since reincarnation involves a physical body and returning to the same plane of existence). We will all be "saved" as we gradually leave our material beliefs behind and realize our true spirituality. In Christian Science, our salvation is not from eternal damnation, but from our belief in materiality.

Notes

1 Mary Baker Eddy, *Science and Health with Key to the Scriptures* (Boston: Published by the Trustees under the Will of Mary Baker G. Eddy, 1934), 587:5-8.

2 Mrs. Eddy defines "mortal mind" as "Nothing claiming to be something . . . the belief that sensation is in matter, which is sensationless; a belief that life, substance, and intelligence are in and of matter; the opposite of Spirit, and therefore the opposite of God, or good; the belief that life has a beginning and therefore an end; the belief that man is the offspring of mortals; the belief that there can be more than one creator; . . . material senses; . . . sin; sickness; death." (*Science and Health* 591:25-592:10)

3 Mary Baker Eddy, *Science and Health,* 591:8-9, 13-15.

4 Ibid., 468:9-10, 14-15.

5 Mary Baker Eddy, "Principle and Practice," *Christian Science Sentinel* 20:1 (1917):10.

6 Mary Baker Eddy, *Science and Health,* 107:1-6.

7 Ibid., 368:27-31.

8 Annie Knott, "Reminiscences of Mary Baker Eddy," *We Knew Mary Baker Eddy,* 3rd series (Boston: The Christian Science Publishing Society, 1953): 86-87.

CHAPTER THREE
Source Materials:
Who is Telling the Truth?

The early history of Christian Science is fraught with triumphs, storms, and intrigue. Sometimes it reads like a thriller novel, while at other times it sinks to the level of a soap opera. The meaning of many events is open to a wide variety of interpretations, often based upon which interviews one chooses to believe and on whether or not one is a Christian Scientist. This is not unusual; any event may be viewed differently by its various participants and witnesses, depending upon their vantage points, preconceived ideas, and roles in the incident. By interviewing several of the people involved, it is usually possible to find a thread of truth that generally describes the event. I have used this tactic in trying to present an accurate view of Mary Baker Eddy and her religious movement.

The research for this book is gleaned from a number of sources. Most of them can be considered "pro-Christian Science," although the writings sympathetic to Christian Science include literature both authorized and not authorized by the Church.[1] I have also studied some of what Christian Scientists consider to be negative literature in order to achieve a sense of balance. This balance is very important since most of what Christian Scientists read of their religion is officially sanctioned by the Church. My primary sources include the following:

Robert Peel's trilogy *Mary Baker Eddy: The Years of Discovery,*[2] *The Years of Trial,*[3] and *The Years of Authority.*[4] Written in the late 1960s and early 1970s, this biography is considered by Christian Scientists to be one of the most scholarly and unbiased biographies available. Peel was a Christian Scientist and his series is Church-authorized. During the late 1970s I studied these books in detail as part of a college course entitled "The History of the Christian Science Movement" (I attended a college for Christian Scientists). I still have my class notes and used them extensively during my research for this book in order to guide me to pertinent sections of the Peel books. My class notes also contain notes from several other "Church approved" books I will not list here.

Persistent Pilgrim: The Life of Mary Baker Eddy, by Richard A Nenneman.[5] Nenneman converted to Christian Science as an adult. In addition to other church-related positions, he was editor-in-chief of the international newspaper, *The Christian Science Monitor,* from 1988 to 1992. The Christian Science Board of Directors gave Nenneman complete access to the archives of the Church History Department in order to gather material for his book. This allowed him to read both Mrs. Eddy's personal correspondence (including over 10,000 letters) and also the personal reminiscences of many who knew her. Using this information, he wrote a very interesting and supportive biography which the Christian Science Publishing Society decided not to publish (but did later authorize). While wholeheartedly supporting the idea that Mrs. Eddy's leadership is divinely ordained, Nenneman examines her human side as she develops into a spiritual leader and runs her church. Nenneman has an interesting perspective; as a convert, he acknowledges that Christian Science absolutely defies standard logic.[6] He devotes several pages to the spiritual logic behind Christian Science and also to Mrs. Eddy's use of language.

Mary Baker Eddy: Christian Healer, by Yvonne Caché von Fettweis and Robert Townsend Warneck.[7] Von Fettweis is a Christian Science practitioner (professional healer) and has worked at The Mother Church[8] for over thirty years, primarily with the Church's historical collections. She became Church Historian in 1995. Warneck has worked at The Mother

Church for over twenty-four years, both in the Board of Directors' office and in the Church History Department. Von Fettweis and Warneck gleaned their material from the research of former archivists, from more than 21,000 of Mrs. Eddy's unpublished letters and writings, and from the recorded memories of people who knew her. Unlike Peel's and Nenneman's works, which attempt to give a balanced view of Mrs. Eddy, I find von Fettweis and Warneck's Church-authorized biography to be hopelessly biased. The book overemphasizes Mrs. Eddy's positive qualities while glossing over problems discussed in the other biographies. It bombards the reader with her healing work and her love, painting her much larger than life. It also perpetuates the traditions and myths taught to all Christian Science children, like the myth that Mrs. Eddy experienced an immediate and lasting healing three days after her famous fall on the ice (Chapter 4).

The personal memoirs of Adam Dickey[9] and Judge Septimus Hanna,[10] two of Mrs. Eddy's "inner circle" and most ardent supporters. These manuscripts were not published by the Publishing Society although Mrs. Eddy specifically asked Dickey to write his memoirs about the time he spent in her household. Dickey died before finishing the memoirs and his wife published the unfinished manuscript. The Church suppressed the manuscript and buried it in the Church archives—I suspect because Dickey revealed a little too much about life in Mrs. Eddy's household.

The *We Knew Mary Baker Eddy Series.*[11] These Church-authorized books contain the personal reminiscences of eighteen Christian Scientists who spent time with Mrs. Eddy. Many of these people helped form the backbone of her religious movement.

Mrs. Eddy's own writings, including *Science and Health with Key to the Scriptures, Prose Works,* and *The Manual of The Mother Church.*[12] *Science and Health* contains the basic teachings of Christian Science and is considered the religion's "textbook." *Prose Works* is a compilation of Mrs. Eddy's other major published writings, including *Miscellaneous Writings; Retrospection and Introspection; Unity of Good; Pulpit and Press; Rudimental Divine Science; No and Yes; Christian Science versus Pantheism;*

her *Message[s] to The Mother Church* for 1900, 1901, and 1902; *Christian Healing; The People's Idea of God;* and *The First Church of Christ, Scientist and Miscellany. The Manual* contains by-laws for The Mother Church and policies that affect all Christian Science churches.

The Destiny of The Mother Church by Bliss Knapp.[13] Bliss Knapp and his parents were part of Mrs. Eddy's inner circle. The Board of Directors refused to publish this book for over 40 years, presumably because it deals heavily with Mrs. Eddy's role in biblical prophecy and, in some people's opinions, comes dangerously close to deifying her. In desperate need of money, the Publishing Society decided to publish the book in 1991, as Mr. Knapp had cleverly promised the Christian Science Church an estate worth over $90 million for its publication.

The Life of Mary Baker G. Eddy and the History of Christian Science by Willa Cather and Georgine Milmine.[14] This biography was first published as a series of articles in *McClure's* magazine in 1907 and 1908. The series was re-published as a book in 1909. It is the only "anti- Christian Science" biography I used, although I question whether it really intends to discredit Christian Science or is just too close to the truth in many of the incidents it describes.

Peel spends a great deal of effort refuting this book in his trilogy, and I was taught that the book was nothing but cheap yellow journalism. It was quickly suppressed by the Christian Scientists after it was published in 1909 but was republished in 1993. The biography is actually fascinating and agrees, in basic substance (but perhaps not in interpretation), with much of what is in the "pro-Eddy" biographies. Milmine was originally cited as the author of the articles and book, but it was later discovered that Cather probably wrote the articles and book from research that Milmine gathered.

Blue Windows: A Christian Science Childhood by Barbara Wilson.[15] Barbara Wilson, a contemporary author and feminist, published her memoirs in *Blue Windows*. In this heart-wrenching book, Wilson does a remarkable job of describing what it feels like to be a Christian Science child. She captures the beautiful side of Christian Science, the emotional grip this religion can have on people, and the confusion and tragedy of a healing-gone-wrong. This book is a "must-read" for anyone who is confused and troubled by aspects of his or her Christian Science background and needs to feel that he or she is not alone.

Notes

1 The Christian Science Publishing Society publishes official Christian Science literature, thereby deciding what information is authorized (i.e., acceptable) and what is not authorized.

2 Robert Peel, *Mary Baker Eddy: The Years of Discovery* (New York: Holt, Rinehart & Winston, 1966).

3 Robert Peel, *Mary Baker Eddy: The Years of Trial* (New York: Holt, Rinehart & Winston, 1971).

4 Robert Peel, *Mary Baker Eddy: The Years of Authority* (Boston: The Christian Science Publishing Society, 1977).

5 Richard A. Nenneman, *Persistent Pilgrim: The Life of Mary Baker Eddy* (Etna, NH: Nebbadoon Press, 1997).

6 Nenneman comments that the religion requires "a complete laying aside of the deeply held human belief in a material creation and a mortal man—the common sense view of life" (173). He later comments that Christian Science treatment requires "seeing the universe as God sees it— spiritual and perfect—a viewpoint that in every detail contradicts the evidence of our senses" (195).

7 Yvonne Caché von Fettweis and Robert Townsend Warneck, *Mary Baker Eddy: Christian Healer* (Boston: The Christian Science Publishing Society, 1998).

8 The Mother Church is the familiar name for The First Church of Christ, Scientist, Boston, Massachusetts. The Church's world headquarters and Publishing Society are located on the grounds of The Mother Church.

9 Adam H. Dickey, *Memoirs of Mary Baker Eddy* (1927; reprint, Santa Clarita, CA: The Bookmark, n.d.).

10 Judge Septimus J. Hanna and Camilla Hanna, *Reminiscences of Mary Baker Eddy* (reprint, Santa Clarita, CA: The Bookmark, n.d.).

11 *We Knew Mary Baker Eddy, Series 1-4* (Boston: The Christian Science Publishing Society, 1943-1972).

12 Mrs. Eddy's writings can be obtained from the Christian Science Publishing Society in Boston, Massachusetts. They are also available at Reading Rooms maintained by individual Christian Science Churches.

13 Bliss Knapp, *The Destiny of The Mother Church* (1947; reprint, Boston: The Christian Science Publishing Society, 1991).

14 Willa Cather and Georgine Milmine, *The Life of Mary Baker G. Eddy & the History of Christian Science* (1909; reprint, Lincoln: University of Nebraska Press, 1993).

15 Barbara Wilson, *Blue Windows: A Christian Science Childhood* (New York: Picador USA, 1997).

CHAPTER FOUR
A Remarkable Woman

Why study Mary Baker Eddy when evaluating Christian Science? Because she said that we must know her to understand her religion. She discouraged personality worship and claimed to have merely been God's scribe, but she emphasized that one can understand Christian Science only through a clear understanding of her. Consider the following comments:

> All the people need, in order to love and adopt Christian Science, is the true sense of its Founder. In proportion as they have it, will our Cause advance[1] (Mary Baker Eddy, 1899).

> ... no one knows anything of Christian Science except as it has come through her. ... we must never permit our Leader to be separated in our thought from her teachings[2] (Bliss Knapp's comments to Mrs. Eddy, of which she approved).

> Our Leader encourages us to seek and find her in her writings. The hostility of mortal mind endeavors to separate her from her writings and so keep us from more intimate communion with her. Perhaps we sometimes read *Science and Health* without a thought of the author. May we not rather realize

that we are not only reading the word of God, but that our communion with Him is through the message written by His chosen scribe?[3] (Daisette McKenzie)

Christian Science is my only ideal; and the individual and his ideal can never be severed. If either is misunderstood or maligned, it eclipses the other with the shadow cast by this error[4] (Mrs. Eddy).

These comments suggest that it is crucial to know Mrs. Eddy in order to understand the religion she founded.

Mrs. Eddy preferred to be understood through her writings. Yet, because she was a leader, it is also important to observe her leadership style and the way that her followers responded to her (the Church apparently agrees with this approach since it has authorized several biographies). Understanding the writings, the leader, and the followers will provide our best chance at understanding why Christian Science attracts people and how it affects them.

I will briefly look at Mrs. Eddy's personal history. I will then examine her personality, her leadership style, and how she and others viewed her role in Christianity. This multi-pronged approach should help explain this remarkable woman.

A Brief History

Mary Baker was born in 1821 in the rural town of Bow, New Hampshire. She was the youngest in a family of six children. Her father was a strict and outspoken Calvinist who believed in predestination and the wrath of God. Her mother believed in a God of unconditional love.[5] Mary grew up sandwiched between these two modes of religious thought. She rejected the idea of predestination early in life and was courageous enough to defend her beliefs in front of the elders of her family's Congregational Church. Sometime during her adolescent or teenage years, she was accepted into the church despite her disagreement with its elders over this fundamental doctrinal issue.[6]

Mary struggled with poor health throughout her childhood and adult years. Cather states that she was "subject from infancy to convulsive attacks of a hysterical nature" and that, between her nervous condition and her strong will, she quickly gained dominance over the otherwise well-ordered household. Cather adds:

> These evidences of an abnormal condition of the nerves are important to any study of Mrs. Eddy and her career. As child and woman she suffered from this condition, and its existence explains some phases of her nature and certain of her acts, which otherwise might be difficult to understand and impossible to estimate.[7]

Nenneman also refers to an "unfortunate susceptibility to illness." He continues,

> To some degree this has to be understood as a phenomenon of that period, or of any period in which religious emotionalism is allowed to become confused with religious commitment. . . . Mary was more than normally sensitive to the thoughts of those around her. . . . Whether or not the kind of sensitivity she had as a child had any relation to her various illnesses, it is a fact that her health became a nagging problem.[8]

Peel also discusses Mary's childhood illnesses and suggests that one of their causes might have been her religious disagreements with her father.[9] Nenneman mentions that Mary's physical ailments worsened when her adolescent son moved to Minnesota with the family that raised him.[10]

It is interesting that all three biographers suggest that at least some of Mary's health problems may have had emotional connections and, according to Cather, a possible neurological etiology. Some of her other ills included dyspepsia (indigestion) and back pain, both of which are often related to stress. The emotional connection becomes clear as one examines later events in her life.

Mary Baker married George Glover in December of 1843. The couple soon moved to North Carolina. George died of yellow fever six months after their marriage, leaving Mary pregnant with their son George. Mary then moved back to her parents' home in Sanbornton Bridge, New Hampshire. Her mother died in 1849. Her father remarried in 1850, at which point Mary moved in with her sister Abigail Tilton and her family. Shortly thereafter, Mary's son went to live with a neighbor named Mahala Sanborn.

There is some dispute over whether the child was taken from Mary or whether she willingly allowed him to leave. Cather states that Mahala and Mary's family cared for George throughout most of his early years and offers a comment from Mary's father that she was like "an old ewe that won't own its lamb."[11] Cather suggests that this lack of interest in her son may have been a symptom of a nervous disorder:

> The symptoms of serious nervous disorder so conspicuous in Mrs. Eddy's young womanhood—the exaggerated hysteria, the anesthesia, the mania for being rocked and swung—are sometimes accompanied by a lack of maternal feeling, and the absence of it in Mrs. Eddy must be considered, like her lack of the sense of smell, a defect of constitution rather than a vice of character.[12]

Christian Scientists vehemently deny that Mary ignored her son and that she had neurological or emotional disorders. They do acknowledge that her frequent illness set the tone of her adult life as she searched for a means to overcome her difficulties.

Mary's search for health extended into the 1860s, during which she met Dr. Phineas B. Quimby and also began to develop her Christian Science doctrine. The years between 1844 and the 1860s are rather bleak, punctuated by a failed thirteen-year marriage to Dr. Daniel Patterson and years of living from house to house as a boarder or with friends. Throughout this time, she experimented with various healing methods which failed to significantly improve her health.

In October of 1862, Mrs. Eddy received her first treatment from Phineas Quimby. Dr. Quimby believed that much of his patients' ability to get well lay in their *belief* in their doctor's ability to help them. In treating the sick, he used a combination of talking to them and performing a few manipulations, such as wetting a woman's hair or rubbing a person's head to help the flow of electricity in his or her body (a belief held by mesmerists of the day).[13] In any case, Mrs. Eddy was greatly helped by Quimby's treatment and became a firm believer in his healing method. She and a few other followers spent a great deal of time talking with him and copying his manuscripts with his permission. She later taught the Quimby method of healing before establishing the religion she called Christian Science.

There has been much controversy regarding Quimby's role in Christian Science. Many have claimed that Mrs. Eddy used some of Quimby's ideas and even plagiarized his writings as she developed her religion. This is a serious accusation since Mrs. Eddy maintained that Christian Science was a revelation straight from God. Despite its importance, the "Quimby controversy" will not be detailed in this book because it is so volatile that it would distract from the book's real emphasis. The truth regarding Quimby's alleged role in Christian Science doctrine is important but not critical to the general discussion of Christian Science and mind control. Readers interested in the issue can find it discussed in the Peel, Nenneman, and Cather biographies, as well as in numerous other works on Christian Science.

Nenneman points out some of Quimby's positive and non-controversial influences on Mrs. Eddy. He appreciated her intellect and took her seriously, giving her a sense of confidence that helped her emerge from her "semi-invalidism" of the 1850s. By 1866, she finally had a purpose in life and "was in search of something that, while it still eluded her, she had become determined to find."[14] In 1907, she said,

> I tried him [Quimby], as a healer, and because he seemed to
> help me for the time, and had a higher ideal than I had heard
> of up to that time, I praised him to the skies . . . I actually loved

> him, I mean his high and noble character, and was literally un-
> stinted in my praise of him, but when I found that Quimbyism
> was too short, and would not answer the cry of the human
> heart for succor, for real aid, I went, being driven thence by
> my extremity, to the Bible, and there I discovered Christian
> Science.[15]

Phineas Quimby died on 16 January 1866. Two weeks later, Mrs. Eddy fell on the ice and was injured. Every Christian Science child is taught that Mrs. Eddy was expected to die but that she found healing through reading the Bible. On the third day she arose from her bed, healed and free.[16] In referring to the event as the beginning of her discovery of Christian Science, Mrs. Eddy describes the injury "that neither medicine nor surgery could reach." She calls her recovery "immediate" and describes it as "the falling apple that led me to the discovery how to be well myself, and how to make others so."[17] This injury and healing are thus considered by most Christian Scientists to mark the "official" discovery of Christian Science. Believers are taught (and are told by Mrs. Eddy's writings)[18] that she then embarked on a three-year journey into the Bible during which God revealed to her the fundamentals of Christian Science. The whole process sounds both heavenly and straightforward. Mrs. Eddy and the Church fail to mention that she experienced recurring problems from the accident—several *months* later she tried to extract money from the city for her injuries, on the grounds that she was still suffering.[19] They also downplay the difficult and often stormy events that accompanied the establishment of Christian Science.

Charisma

How would you feel if you were privileged to spend time with:
"the greatest benefactor to humanity that has lived since the time of Jesus . . . ,"[20] "God's chosen scribe,"[21] "a reflection of ever-present Truth,"[22] the one who "brought to mankind the Comforter of which [Jesus] spoke,"[23] the "perfect blending of the spiritual and practical,"

showing what makes a "real" Christian Scientist,[24] someone who could either read people's thoughts or had exceptional discernment,[25] a person who lived in the "home of Truth" as the one whom God had called,[26] someone "above human praise or criticism," whose judgment was "as near to perfection as is possible in this world,"[27] the most gentle, courteous, and meek person you have ever met,[28] "refinement itself,"[29] someone whose presence brought inspiration, and whose "ring of sincerity . . . held her listeners spellbound . . . ,"[30] someone with remarkable eyes which "looked out beyond the human sense of things into spiritual realities,"[31] a person who "lived in perfect harmony with life,"[32] a teacher whose daily Bible lessons were like manna from heaven, and with whom a conversation could leave an impression "not unlike what the disciples must have felt on the mount of transfiguration"?[33]

The above descriptions refer to Mary Baker Eddy. All but two are from the Church-authorized book series, *We Knew Mary Baker Eddy,* which contains the speeches and writings of eighteen Christian Scientists who knew their leader personally. The series supports the Church's official image of its leader and depicts her as a wonderful, strong, caring, spiritually gifted woman. The passion she kindled among her followers is illustrated by their reaction to a speech she delivered in 1888:

> Up came the crowds to her side, begging for one hand-clasp, one look, one memorial of her, *whose name was a power and a sacred thing in their homes. . . .*[34] (emphasis added)

"A sacred thing in their homes"—what an illuminating phrase.

Despite the above descriptions, even some of the sympathetic memoirs and biographies suggest that Mrs. Eddy was not as wonderful as her official image might suggest. Sprinkled throughout these writings are statements, or at least hints, that her temper and perfectionism could make her rather difficult. Calvin Hill comments that Mrs. Eddy had difficulty keeping a full staff of workers in her home.[35] Nenneman mentions that, while in her mid-sixties, Mrs. Eddy was still learning to practice "gentleness" with outsiders.[36] He also states that, as she identified herself as mortal mind's focal point in attacking Christian Science, "she expressed herself in increasingly strong and authoritative language to her followers and, sometimes, probably stepped beyond the bounds of what she would have liked to be remembered for."[37] Several students who left her in 1881 cited "frequent ebullitions of temper, love of money, and the appearance of hypocrisy" as reasons they could no longer follow her.[38]

Despite her shortcomings, Mrs. Eddy possessed true charisma. Cather describes the phenomenon in the following excerpts:

> Mrs. Crosby . . . gives an interesting account of [Mrs. Patterson's] visit [in 1864] which lasted several months. Mrs. Patterson, she says, although in a state of almost absolute destitution, retained the air of a grand lady which had so characterized her in her youth. Although visiting at a farmhouse where every one had a part in the household duties, Mrs. Patterson was always the guest of honor, nor did it occur to any one to suggest her sharing the daily routine. Mrs. Crosby's servants waited upon the guest, and even her room was cared for by others. . . . Mrs. Crosby admits that she was completely under Mrs. Patterson's spell, and says that even after years of estrangement and complete disillusionment, she still feels that Mrs. Patterson was the most stimulating and invigorating influence she has ever known. Like all of Mrs. Eddy's old intimates, she speaks of their days of companionship with a certain shade of regret—as if life in the society of this woman was more intense and keen than it ever was afterward.[39]

> All these people with whom she once stayed, love to talk of her, and most of them are glad to have known her,—even those who now say that the experience was a costly one. She was like a patch of color in those gray communities. She was never dull . . . and never commonplace. She never laid aside her regal air; never entered a room or left it like other people. There was something about her that continually excited and

stimulated, and she gave people the feeling that a great deal was happening.[40]

Mrs. Eddy was truly remarkable. While in her mid-forties, she rose from ill health and difficult personal circumstances to become a multimillionaire and the leader of a major religious movement in a society dominated by men. She commanded tremendous respect and loyalty among her followers. Whether through positive or negative circumstances, something about her captured the imagination of those who knew her. She possessed a charisma that deeply affected people—through attraction, repulsion, or a strange mixture of the two.

Unquestioned Authority

There is a difference between authoritative and authoritarian leadership. Authoritative leaders gain their power through legitimate means, such as election or experience. They are in some way accountable to their subordinates and can be removed from power if they misuse their authority.

In contrast, authoritarian leaders may or may not gain their power through legitimate means. They claim absolute authority and immunity from accountability. Authoritarian leaders demand unhesitating, unquestioning obedience from their subordinates. To justify this leadership style they often claim divinity, direct revelation from God, or some other kind of special knowledge.

Mrs. Eddy was an authoritarian leader. Her style becomes apparent when studying how she interacted with her inner circle of workers and with Christian Scientists in general. It is also revealed by the way she and her followers spiritually justified her decisions and behavior, whether or not they seemed wise or appropriate.

When studying Mrs. Eddy's leadership style it is important to first address her repeated statement, "Follow your Leader, only so far as she follows Christ."[41] This challenge to "follow me only as long as I act appropriately" implies that she did not want to misuse her power and might seem to refute the claim that she was an authoritarian leader. Her statement is, however, typical of both types of leaders. While an authoritative leader makes the statement sincerely, it has little meaning when uttered by an authoritarian leader. The authoritarian leader has placed constraints upon his or her group which make it difficult for followers to critically evaluate the "rightness" of their leader's actions.

Listed below are some quotes and anecdotes illustrating Mrs. Eddy's leadership style. They show that she claimed absolute and unquestioned authority as the founder and discoverer of Christian Science. The quotes are taken from her biographies and from several of her most loyal followers. Unless otherwise stated, all italicized phrases represent my emphasis.

Regarding leadership:

> She told me that every government, every organization . . . must have one responsible head. This is why *she placed herself at the head of her own Church, because the mortal mind could not be trusted to conduct it.* This is why she did away with First Members, and later Executive Members, for to place enactments of holy inspiration in the hands of groups of individuals was to incur the possibility of the Divine idea being lost sight of, and human wisdom taking its place. *This is also why she reduced the authority of the conduct of The Mother Church into the narrowest possible compass.* Indeed, she told me, with pathos and earnestness, that if she could find one individual, who was spiritually equipped, she would immediately place him at the head of her church government. Asking me to take a pencil she slowly dictated the following . . . "I prayed God day and night to show me how to form my Church, and how to go on with it. I understand that He showed me, just as I understand He showed me Christian Science, and no human being ever showed me Christian Science. Then *I have no right or desire to change what God has directed me to do, and it remains for the Church to obey it.* What has prospered this Church for thirty years will continue to keep it" (Adam Dickey).[42]

Mr. and Mrs. Eddy left Boston for an extended trip to Washington, D.C. and Philadelphia during the winter of 1882. Mrs. Eddy left Julia Bartlett in charge of affairs in Boston, with the comment,

> There should be a substitute for me to lead this people and now dear Student, I ask you will you take this place *not that you can unloose the sandals of my shoes not that you can fill my place but only that I think you rather more fit for it than anyone whom I leave.* Now do not yield to temptation and say you cannot. . . .

Nenneman remarks that the statement would have been "baffling" to anyone less humble than Bartlett.[43] Baffling? How about demeaning, insulting, rude, arrogant, tactless . . .

On making mistakes:
> . . . *it seems that* the changing of her mind was a privilege that our Leader reserved for herself, *and she exercised it without any regard whatever for what had gone before. . . . Then* she said to me, *"Mr. Dickey, people say that I am changeable,—that I change my mind frequently, but when I do,* it is always God that changes me. . . . I would not condemn myself, therefore, for what seemed a mistake, but would include it as part of the working out of the problem" (*Adam Dickey*).[44]

Compare the above quote with the next set of comments regarding Mrs. Eddy and mistakes.

> Often the reasons for which our Leader took action in certain directions were not clear to the workers about her. It would seem as if the reason advanced by her was a poor one. . . . *This, of course, was mortal mind's analysis of her work.* . . . It always turned out, however, that her action was right, *regardless of the reason assigned,* which convinced those who were familiar

with her work that *her judgment was unerring in every detail,*
and that in following the direction of divine Wisdom, *she never
made a mistake. Often I heard her say with great impressiveness
that in over forty years of church leadership, she had not made a
mistake, a record that is most truly remarkable* (Adam Dickey).[45]

Nenneman comments that Mrs. Eddy "did not make a habit of saying
she had made mistakes. That she took many risks, she would admit."[46]
Apparently Mrs. Eddy justified her claim of never making mistakes by
simply defining a mistake as a risk that did not work out.

Concerning obedience:

Christian Scientists owe much gratitude to the little band of
workers who *loyally and unhesitatingly followed and obeyed
our Leader* in those early endeavors to prove the teachings of Christ Jesus in healing the sick and destroying sin.
(Annie Robertson)[47]

She made known to her students the needs of the hour and
the snares and pitfalls that lay in our path in our warfare
against error and how to avoid them. *Happy was the student
who obeyed her instruction, for in obedience to her teachings
was his salvation, and through disobedience many lost their
way.* (Julia Bartlett)[48]

Within a few weeks after the Normal class of February, 1887,
I received a letter from Mrs. Eddy inviting me to be present at a meeting of students to be held April 13. . . . I felt
that I could not well spare the time or money to return to
Boston [from the Midwest] so soon . . . and wrote her to
that effect. (I afterwards learned that the majority of those
who had been asked to come on for this gathering had sent
our Leader word that they would be unable to comply. . . .)
Within a short time . . . there was delivered to me . . . the

following letter from Mrs. Eddy . . . "I have gotten up this N.C.S.A. [National Christian Scientist Association] for you and the life of the Cause. *I have something important to say to you, a message from God. Will you not meet this one request of your teacher and let* nothing *hinder it? If you do not I shall never make another to you and give up the struggle. . . ."* It is needless to say that this message from our Leader *dispelled the thought which was seeking to hinder students* from responding to their teacher's request. . . . the experience has always been remembered as a vital step in my progress. . . . I also learned on this occasion the lesson which we need to think upon many times, that *simple obedience to any righteous requirement in our Cause brings unstinted reward* (Annie Knott).[49]

"Experience, and above all, obedience, are the tests of growth and understanding in Science," Mrs. Eddy wrote to her students in the *Journal.* . . . Mrs. Eddy's direct personal control of the Boston church soon meant the direct personal control of a membership reaching from Maine to California.[50]

In 1901, Mrs. Eddy invited Mrs. Stewart for a private interview and added:

Tell her that *her prompt obedience to the call will ensure to her life, health, and heaven.*[51]

Mary Baker Eddy, to the last class she taught and which she called at the last minute, bringing students from unreasonably long distances for such short notice:

Your prompt presence in Concord at my unexplained call witnesses your fidelity to Christian Science and your spiritual unity with your Leader.[52]

At the first annual meeting of The Mother Church, Dr. Foster Eddy told the people:

> We have come to the time when all should listen to the voice of Love, and hearing it, *we should follow implicitly whether we understand or not,* and the way will be made plain.[53]

> "What," asked the Rev. D.A. Easton, pastor of The Mother Church, in his Easter sermon, 1893, *"what does membership in The Mother Church mean? It signifies obedience.* Mrs. Eddy has invited Scientists everywhere to unite with The Mother Church. *To obey cheerfully and loyally marks a growth in Science. 'Theirs is not to reason why, Theirs is but to do and die.'* "[54]

It makes sense that Mrs. Eddy would consider her leadership to be above question. She believed that Christian Science was divinely revealed to *her.* Since she was the one to whom God revealed His inspired interpretation of the Bible and this "scientific" system of healing, it made sense to her that she should be the undisputed leader of the church, its policies, and its doctrine. Successful and consistent healing required absolute adherence to the method that God had given her. In effect, her followers had to learn to think as she taught them to think, because she had learned how to think from God. Disobedience to her doctrine meant disobedience to God and was, in fact, labeled as immorality.[55] Cather reports that Mrs. Eddy had one argument that always made her victorious in business disagreements. She "would draw up her shoulders, look her opponent in the eye, and say very slowly, 'God has directed me in this matter. Have you anything further to say?'"[56]

Aside from what she considered to be her God-ordained authority, Mrs. Eddy seems to have had a real need to control whatever situation she might encounter. Cather, Peel, and Nenneman all describe or at least strongly hint at her temper and perfectionism.[57] These, together with her charisma and tendency to retain an air of grandeur despite her circumstances, suggest a woman who very much wanted to have things her way and to be the center of attention. Two illustrations will show her intense desire for control and order:

The first subject involves perfectionism. Mrs. Eddy's need for perfect order is described both in her biographies and in her students' memoirs. During her later years she had a full time staff of Christian Scientists living with her and taking care of her house, assisting with her business responsibilities, and acting as spiritual body guards against the attacks of malicious animal magnetism (evil thoughts which could hurt and even kill a person—see Chapter 7, Animal Magnetism). In his memoirs, Adam Dickey describes how difficult it was to find and maintain such a staff of workers. First of all, these people had to be successful Christian Scientists who had never been incapacitated, even though they might now be in perfect health. They had to be willing to follow Mrs. Eddy's orders implicitly and to be available on a moment's notice.

During the time they lived in Mrs. Eddy's household, the workers' lives revolved completely around her and her absolutely precise way of doing things. Dickey points out that "orderliness, neatness, and dispatch were among the leading characteristics of our Leader." For example, he describes the difficulty her housekeepers experienced every time they dusted. She would become irritated if everything was not replaced *exactly* as it had been before the room was cleaned. He continues,

> In order, then, that no mistakes should be made and that they might not yield to *the argument of error that they could not please Mrs. Eddy,* a tiny brass tack was driven into the floor through the carpet, marking the place where each piece of furniture belonged. . . . (emphasis added).

Mr. Dickey uses Christian Science logic to justify this excessive need for orderliness:

> . . . her room represented to her a condition of thought. . . .
> To her every picture, every ornament, and piece of furniture
> in her rooms represented a thought, and when these were

> rightly adjusted, her thought was undisturbed. . . . This illus-
> trated the fact that, even in such a simple thing as sweeping a
> room and rearranging the furniture, the following of a definite
> rule of Principle makes everything easier.[58]

It is not surprising that when Mrs. Eddy bought new carpets for the workers' bedrooms in 1899 and gave everyone a choice of color, each of them declined the privilege and asked Mrs. Eddy to make the decision.[59]

Calvin Hill had the job of searching the country for workers who could fulfill Mrs. Eddy's requirements (finally, a committee of three was selected for this purpose). He points out in his writings that many of Mrs. Eddy's workers soon lost their joy and spiritual vision, and that she had difficulty maintaining a full staff.[60]

A second illustration of her need for control involves a series of students she taught during the early years of Christian Science. She had few followers during the 1860s and 1870s. A few favorites stand out among these early students—"right hand men," one might say, who showed an extra measure of faithfulness to Mrs. Eddy and service to the Cause. The first of these was Richard Kennedy, with whom she went into business in 1870. Mrs. Eddy held classes while Mr. Kennedy developed a successful healing practice using Mrs. Eddy's principles. This arrangement lasted less than two years before they dissolved their partnership. One of their major disagreements centered on Kennedy's practice of rubbing his patients' heads as he treated them. Mrs. Eddy had, at one time, used this practice as Quimby had before her, but had abandoned it as she tried to separate herself from Quimby's methods and from what she now considered to be his use of mesmerism. When Kennedy refused to change his healing techniques, Mrs. Eddy labeled him a mesmerist and turned him into the movement's greatest enemy. He was, one might say, the "great Satan," and became the scapegoat for any negative occurrence in Mrs. Eddy's cause. Since Christian Scientists believe that negative thoughts can harm, Kennedy seemed to have tremendous power to wreak havoc within the little band of followers. He was blamed for illness, defections, and all manner of problems. Mrs. Eddy soon had a new favorite named

Daniel Spofford, who later also broke with her and was immediately labeled a mesmerist. Spofford was followed by Edward Arens, whom she eventually accused of mentally poisoning her husband. And so continued the string of favorites who eventually fell out of favor, were labeled as mesmerists, and were turned into enemies. This trend continued over the years although Mrs. Eddy gradually began to view mesmerism more as an impersonal evil than as the work of individuals. Her adopted son Ebenezer J. Foster fell from favor in the late 1880s, showing how long this trend continued.

Cather offers some interesting comments regarding Mrs. Eddy's habit of becoming very close to a student and then experiencing an emotionally violent break with the person. Cather's analysis supports the profile of an authoritarian leader who constantly needs to be in control. The analysis is best presented in two segments: the first relating to a specific student, and the second relating to Mrs. Eddy's general need for control. All italicized words represent my emphasis:

> Although no open rupture occurred between Mrs. Eddy and Daniel Spofford until the summer of 1877, by the spring of 1877 Mrs. Eddy's feeling for him had begun to cool. It will be remembered that she had turned a number of her students over to Mr. Spofford for instruction. . . . As a teacher, Mr. Spofford proved so popular that Mrs. Eddy repented the authority she had given him. His success in practice also made her restive,— doubtless one of the causes which led her to insist upon his turning his practice over to Asa Gilbert Eddy and devoting his time to pushing the sale of her book. It would be scarcely fair to draw the conclusion that Mrs. Eddy resented the success of her students in itself, *but she certainly looked upon it with apprehension if the student showed any inclination to adopt methods of his own or to think for himself. Mrs. Eddy required of her students absolute and unquestioning conformity to her wishes; any other attitude of mind she regarded as dangerous.* She often told Mr. Spofford that there was no such thing as devotion to

the principle of revealed truth which did not include devotion to the revelator. *"I am Wisdom, and this revelation is mine,"* she would declare when a student questioned her decision.[61]

She loved to amaze and astonish; when her students ceased to "wonder," she was usually through with them. Each of her favorites gave her, as it were, a new lease of life; with each one her interest in everything quickened. The great outside audience meant very little as compared with the pliant neophyte beside her chair or across the table from her. *It was when Mrs. Eddy was weaving her spell about a new favorite that she was at her best, and it was then that she most believed in herself. But she could never stop with enchanting, merely. She must altogether absorb the new candidate; he must have nothing left in him which was not from her. If she came upon one insoluble atom hidden away anywhere in the marrow of his bones, she experienced a revulsion and flung him contemptuously aside."*[62]

Cather's unsettling description of one person taking over the personality of another would seem rather unbelievable if it did not so beautifully mesh with modern descriptions of mind control. It is interesting that Cather wrote her comments long before today's theories were developed.

One final subject will be discussed at this time in relation to Mrs. Eddy's leadership style. A leader's style can often be evaluated by the things for which he or she praises or blames subordinates. It is clear from the writers of the *We Knew Mary Baker Eddy* series, as well as from various other writings (including Cather's), that Mrs. Eddy could be charming, encouraging, and generous. Consider, however, some of the things for which she blamed her students:

Her health: Mrs. Eddy often experienced physical symptoms while trying to make important decisions related to the movement. Instead of recognizing the common signs of stress, she blamed her symptoms on the mesmerism of disaffected students working against the cause or on animal magnetism in general.[63]

Her husband's death: An autopsy showed that Mr. Eddy died of heart problems. Mrs. Eddy was shown the damaged heart but still announced that her husband had been murdered by mental arsenic poisoning. She even privately identified the mental assassin as Mr. Arens, one of her disaffected students.[64]

Her nocturnal illnesses: Mrs. Eddy had a staff of workers whose job it was to protect her from mental attack as she slept. If she had a good night's sleep, she praised her students for their successful metaphysical work. If she had problems during the night (which was more often the case), she rebuked her students for failing to "keep their watch," regardless of how diligently they had tried to protect her.[65]

Frequent moves during the early days of the movement: She was often asked to move out soon after taking up residence in a home or boarding house, especially during the winter of 1879-1880. She blamed this misfortune on Kennedy's mesmerism against her instead of considering whether her behavior or other circumstances might have caused the recurring problem.[66]

Defections: Student defections or thoughts against Mrs. Eddy were always assumed to be the work of mesmerists and not the result of her own behavior. In the mass resignation of 1881, some of her most loyal students cited "frequent ebullitions of temper, love of money, and the appearance of hypocrisy" as their reasons for leaving the Christian Scientist Association.[67] Instead of examining her conduct which might have brought on these accusations, Mrs. Eddy blamed her students' dissatisfaction and defection on the work of aggressive mental suggestion emanating from a Mr. Howard.

Her own death: Mrs. Eddy never directly claimed that she would bypass the death experience. She did, however, hold her students spiritually responsible for her demise. This conclusion is clarified by the following explanation: Nenneman points out that she "never felt that her work in firmly establishing the Christian Science movement was entirely finished. In the fall of 1909," he continues, "she wrote that 'the world still needs me here on earth.'"[68] He describes how some of her final writings and letters seem to be good-byes or final instructions to the troops,[69] but apparently fails to recognize the significance of two statements she made to Laura Sargent shortly before her death. On 28 November 1910, she dictated and signed a statement which reads: "It took a combination of sinners that was fast to harm me." A few days later she caught a cold and, sensing the end, commented to Laura, "Oh, if the students had only done what I told them, I should have lived and carried the cause."[70] This statement is consistent with her years of blaming her students for not "keeping their watch" whenever she suffered from her nighttime infirmities. Mrs. Eddy's comments imply that she could have remained on earth to lead her Cause if her students had adequately protected her from the attacks of animal magnetism. Thus, in the final analysis, Mrs. Eddy considered her death to be the result of her students' spiritual failure.

Authoritative leaders do not make the type of demands upon their subordinates that Mrs. Eddy made upon her followers. It follows that, whether or not she was qualified to lead the Christian Science movement in the authoritative sense, her leadership style was definitely authoritarian. Her authoritarianism will become even more obvious as this discussion continues.

Deity and Prophecy

Christians often object to Christian Science because they think that its followers deify Mrs. Eddy. Many Christian Scientists also object to the idea of deifying their leader, as was illustrated by the controversy surrounding the 1991 publication of Ira Knapp's book *The Destiny of The Mother Church*.[71] Knapp had been one of Mrs. Eddy's "inner circle" of followers, but for over forty years the Church refused to publish his book even though he tied his $90 million estate to its publication.[72] One of the reasons for the refusal was that many felt the book came dangerously close to deifying Mrs. Eddy. The Church finally published *The Destiny of The Mother Church* while experiencing serious financial problems, but the book caused dissension within the Church and many Reading Rooms refused to stock it.

Those concerned about deifying Mrs. Eddy are confused by the semantics issue so prevalent in this religion. While traditional Christians consider man to be a physical creation of God, the Christian Scientist views man as a spiritual *reflection* of God and not as His physical creation. It is pointless to worry about deifying the leader of a religion that teaches that we are all the perfect, sinless, spiritual ideas of God. Mrs. Eddy essentially deifies us all with her interpretations of God and Man. Consider the following definitions from the Glossary in *Science and Health*:

> God—The great I AM: the all-knowing, all-seeing, all-acting, all-wise, all-loving, and eternal; Principle; Mind; Soul; Spirit; Life; Truth; Love; all substance; intelligence.[73]

> Man—The compound idea of infinite Spirit; the spiritual image and likeness of God; *the full representation of Mind* (emphasis added).[74]

The Christian Scientist's goal is to prove that he or she is spiritual and perfect—just like God.

I see two issues far more relevant than whether or not Christian Scientists deify their leader. Like deification, these issues address the fundamental question of whether Mrs. Eddy had the spiritual authority to claim divine revelation and to found a "Christian" religion so radically different from traditional Christianity. First is the question of prophecy: do Mrs. Eddy and her followers believe that she is the fulfillment of biblical prophecy? If so, then they must believe that both her writings and her authority are divinely bestowed and that Christian Science is spiritually valid. The second issue involves her relationship to Jesus: Mrs. Eddy claims to reinstate Jesus' healing method, so how does she compare to Him in terms of spirituality and authority? When Mrs. Eddy and Jesus seem to disagree on biblical issues, whom does the Christian Scientist believe?

Prophecy

Mrs. Eddy unmistakably claimed that she and her work were foretold in the Bible. In their Church-authorized biography, von Fettweis and Warneck quote a letter in which she describes her "life-work" as the "theme of ancient prophecy" and herself as "the scribe of His infinite way of Salvation."[75] They also state that Mrs. Eddy's revelation fulfilled Jesus' promise that He would send them a Comforter (John 14:16, 17), that Mrs. Eddy was the "transparency for Truth through which the light of divine Love shown," and that God had prepared her for the revelation.[76]

Mrs. Eddy encouraged her students to believe that she had a specific place in biblical prophecy, as did the Board of Directors in a 1943 editorial entitled "Mrs. Eddy's Place."[77] In the *We Knew Mary Baker Eddy* series, Bliss Knapp states that Mrs. Eddy explained her role in biblical prophecy as did Jesus on the road to Emmaus. Mary Stewart claimed that Mrs. Eddy fulfilled the prophecies of Jesus and John.[78] Judge Septimus Hanna saw her as representing the "female-hood" of God as Jesus had represented the "male-hood" of the "Father Mother God" that Mrs. Eddy described.[79] He also saw her in the barren woman of Isaiah 54[80] and as Jeremiah 4's woman in travail.[81] Hanna and other star pupils like Ira and Bliss Knapp felt that she was the woman of the apocalypse (Rev. 12).

It is instructive to examine Mrs. Eddy's alleged connection to the woman in the apocalypse because it hints at her leadership style and illustrates the power a "divinely sanctioned" leader can command over his or her followers. Mrs. Eddy did not specifically claim to be the woman, but Nenneman mentions that there is no evidence that she corrected her students' misconception.[82] There is, to the contrary, evidence that she quietly encouraged her students in their conclusion. Bliss Knapp describes the moment when his father, Ira, decided that she was the woman. She had just interpreted Revelation 12 to Ira's class when he exclaimed, "Thou art the Woman!" According to Bliss, Mrs. Eddy smiled sweetly at him but "did not rebuke him."[83]

If she did not claim the role, why would a spiritual leader allow herself to be incorrectly (and blasphemously) identified as the woman of the apocalypse? Bliss Knapp provides a compelling reason as he describes the change that occurred in his father once he identified Mrs. Eddy as the woman:

> Although Ira Knapp's knowledge of human nature had taught him never to take any man's word for granted, all this was completely changed in regard to Mrs. Eddy as soon as he had recognized her place in Bible prophecy. He knew that she was God's messenger to this age, one of the two divinely appointed Witnesses. *Then he could never question nor doubt any instruction or requirement which might come to him from God's Witness. In obeying her, he knew that he would be doing God's will,* for Mrs. Eddy said as much to him in several letters which appear later in this book (emphasis added).[84]

In discussing Mrs. Eddy's failure to correct Ira Knapp's declaration that she was the woman, Nenneman comments that Mrs. Eddy "may not have felt a need to correct the statement."[85] Nenneman's conclusion is inconsistent with Mrs. Eddy's need for absolute precision in the teaching and practice of her doctrine and in her private life, and it shows how even a careful writer like Nenneman can fail to recognize manipulation by his spiritual leader.

Mrs. Eddy did finally say that she had *never* thought that she was the woman; she wrote this disclaimer around the time that she was being sued for libel by a disaffected student who accused Mrs. Eddy of calling her the "Babylonish woman" from Revelation. It was apparently no longer convenient to allow the characters in Revelation to represent specific people, so Mrs. Eddy spiritualized the woman of the apocalypse into an illustration of "purity" while claiming that the Babylonish woman represented lust.[86]

Comparison to Jesus

Before observing how Christian Science views its leader in relation to Jesus, it will be helpful to summarize both the Christian Science and traditional Christian concepts of Jesus Christ.

Christian Science separates Christ and Jesus into a dual nature. Mrs. Eddy states:

> Christ is the ideal Truth, that comes to heal sickness and sin through Christian Science, and attributes all power to God. Jesus is the name of the man who, *more than all other men, has presented Christ,* the true idea of God, healing the sick and the sinning and destroying the power of death. Jesus is the human man, and Christ is the divine idea; hence the duality of Jesus the Christ (emphasis added). [87]

In other words, Christian Science teaches that Christ is the divine idea of God (which really represents us all since we are all the perfect ideas of God), while Jesus was a human being and the finest male Christian Scientist ever to walk the earth.

In contrast to Christian Science, the Bible and traditional Christianity make no distinction between Jesus and the Christ. The word "Christ" originates in a Greek term meaning "to anoint,"[88] and represents a title rather than an identity. Jesus Christ means "Jesus, the anointed" rather than pointing to a dual nature. Traditional Christianity teaches that Jesus is divine and part of the Trinity, and that He left heaven and became a perfect man in order to provide the perfect sacrifice for the sins of mankind (See Christian Science and the Bible: Jesus).

Mrs. Eddy did not claim a unique parallel to Christ since she taught that we are *all* perfect reflections of God and are *all* represented by Christ. That is why the question of her deification is immaterial; those who notice parallels drawn between Christ and Mrs. Eddy are really looking at parallels between Christ and all of mankind. Those who find comparisons between Mrs. Eddy and Jesus are seeing parallels drawn to a human being and not to God.

Christian Scientists do, however, draw numerous conscious or unconscious parallels between Mrs. Eddy and Jesus. Many of these comparisons were originated by Mrs. Eddy herself. Identifying Mrs. Eddy with Jesus increases her stature, if not in personality worship (which she avoided), then certainly in spiritual credibility. In observing some of the parallels between Mrs. Eddy and Jesus, we will begin with von Fettweis' and Warneck's Church-authorized biography. According to these authors:

- Mrs. Eddy told her students that when her mother was pregnant with her, she suddenly felt that she was filled with the Holy Spirit and had "dominion over the whole earth." At the same moment, she felt the "quickening of the babe" and began to feel that the child she was carrying was destined for a special, spiritual purpose.[89] Compare this with Mary's foreknowledge of Jesus, with the Holy Spirit's role in Jesus' birth, and to John the Baptist leaping in his mother's womb when the pregnant Mary went to visit John's mother (Luke 1:26-46).
- Mrs. Eddy fell on the ice and was expected to die. She was healed on the third day (33). Jesus rose from the dead on the third day.
- In describing his nomadic ministry style, Jesus commented that "Foxes have holes, and birds of the air have nests; but the Son of man hath no where to lay his head" (Luke 9:58). In 1868, Mrs. Eddy told a friend that she would see the truer meaning of Mrs. Eddy's life if she could understand the spiritual sense of Luke Chapter 9 (39, Ref. 3 p. 405).
- Mrs. Eddy's sister tempted her to give up Christian Science "as [Mrs. Eddy's] Way-shower, Christ Jesus, was tempted in the wilderness" (39), (Matthew 4:1-11).

- Mrs. Eddy experienced opposition from her family. She and her followers compared the opposition to that which Jesus faced in Nazareth (52).
- Mrs. Eddy told Julia Bartlett that she had made herself a servant in order to lead others to Christ (104). Considering the dual nature of Jesus Christ as defined in Christian Science, Jesus also made himself a servant to lead others to Christ.
- In 1882, Mrs. Eddy returned home to a very warm and flamboyant reception after spending several months in Washington D.C. She later wrote to a friend, "this was my entry into Jerusalem. Will it be followed with the cross?" (107).
- The authors state that meekness was one of Mrs. Eddy's "defining qualities" (after extensive research I disagree with their assessment) (164). One of Jesus' defining qualities truly was meekness, as he described himself in Matthew 11:29 and 21:5.
- Both Jesus and Mrs. Eddy claimed that their work was prophesied in the Bible (188, 189; Luke 24:27).
- Von Fettweis and Warneck remark that Mrs. Eddy healed "as Jesus had" (184).

Mrs. Eddy wrote to a student in Chicago:

> For the world to understand me in my true light, and life, would do more for our Cause than aught else could. This I learn from the fact that the enemy ["carnal mind," according to von Fettweis and Warneck] tries harder to hide these two things from the world than to win any other points. *Also Jesus' life and character in their first appearing were treated in like manner* (emphasis added).[90]

Other writers also link Mrs. Eddy to Jesus. When describing Mrs. Eddy's emotional and physical trials, Dickey concludes that she "offered herself as a perpetual sacrifice for the good of humanity" and quotes Isaiah 53:4-5:

Surely he hath borne our griefs, and carried our sorrows: yet we did esteem him stricken, smitten of God, and afflicted. But he was wounded for our transgressions, he was bruised for our iniquities; the chastisement of our peace was upon him; and with his stripes we are healed.[91]

Most Christians assume that this passage from Isaiah 53 refers to Jesus.

One of the most interesting connections between Mrs. Eddy and Jesus involves the Christian Science doctrine regarding His second coming. According to Mrs. Eddy, Jesus' first appearance occurred when His mother understood that "God is the only author of man. . . . Jesus was the offspring of Mary's self-conscious communion with God."[92] Mrs. Eddy declares that "the second appearing of Jesus is, unquestionably, the spiritual advent of the advancing idea of God, as in Christian Science."[93] She attempts to secure her place in spiritual history with the statement:

No person can take the individual place of the Virgin Mary. No person can compass or fulfil the individual mission of Jesus of Nazareth. No person can take the place of the author of Science and Health, the Discoverer and Founder of Christian Science. Each individual must fill his own niche in time and eternity.[94]

An 1888 article in the *Christian Science Journal* expounds upon the issue:

Mary was set apart as the one and only woman who should conceive and bear as she did, whose spiritual sense so arose that she could see man absolutely perfect, the permanent and ever-present expression of Perfection.

Let us come in thought to another day, a day when woman shall commune with God . . . and bring forth the spiritual idea. And what of *her* child? Man is spiritual. Man is mental.

Woman was the first in this day to recognize this, and the other facts it includes. As a result of her communion we have Christian Science.

. . . The realization of Mary, Jesus mother, had a more material expression than at present; but these realizations are alike, in that they are the outcome of conscious communion with God,—the conception of Spirit being reduced to human comprehension.

. . . Divine Science, as we have it today, is the embodiment of our Teacher's spiritual sense, even as Jesus was the embodiment or expression of Mary's sense of Spirit.[95]

One might view Mrs. Eddy's "conception" of Christian Science as a natural process of spiritual evolution, from Mary's physical offspring to Mrs. Eddy's spiritual offspring. In comparing Mrs. Eddy to Jesus, the above passages seem to place Mrs. Eddy a little above Jesus; he was conceived, while she was the one with enough understanding to do the spiritual conceiving.

So, who *does* have more practical significance, day to day, to the Christian Scientist? Whom does the Christian Scientist quote more often, Jesus or Mrs. Eddy? When trying to solve a problem, does the Christian Scientist turn first to the Bible or to *Science and Health?* Whom does the Christian Scientist believe regarding the accuracy of Scripture? The answer to each of these questions rests on the side of Mrs. Eddy and Christian Science. Christian Scientists deeply love Jesus and the Bible but I suggest that, perhaps without realizing it, they are more devoted to Mrs. Eddy and *Science and Health* than to Jesus and the Bible. Most of them would find this statement offensive, but I challenge them to carefully examine their loyalties.

Another event illustrates Mrs. Eddy's relationship to Jesus. After several of her most promising students defected in 1881, her remaining students drafted a set of resolutions which, among other things, declared, "we do understand her to be the chosen messenger of God to bear his truth to the nations, and unless we hear 'Her Voice,' we do not hear 'His Voice.' "[96] Significantly, von Fettweis and Warneck mention that she "edited and approved" the resolutions.[97] Her involvement suggests that she wanted her students to recognize *her* as the avenue to understanding God. But Jesus said, "I am the way, the truth, and the life; no man cometh unto the Father, but by me" (John 14:6). A Christian Scientist might argue that Mrs. Eddy's voice reflected, or spiritually illuminated, Jesus' voice and that Jesus' involvement is implied in the resolution, but this is not true if one studies His words in the Gospels. Jesus spoke of heaven and hell as real places, of judgment as an event and not a process, and of giving Himself to pay for the sins of mankind. Mrs. Eddy reinterpreted Jesus words rather than illuminating them—hearing the voice of Mary Baker Eddy is not the same as hearing the voice of Jesus (see Christian Science and the Bible).

I have examined Mrs. Eddy's background, leadership style, and unusual ability to capture the hearts and imaginations of her students. This analysis was necessary in order to understand Christian Science, as Mrs. Eddy claimed that she could not be separated from her writings and that, to know the writings, one must know the writer. Mrs. Eddy possessed both strengths and flaws, but it is clear that she was a remarkable woman.

Now it is time to address the main subject of this book—mind control. Does Christian Science lock people into modes of thinking that harm them and from which they find it difficult to escape? Let us attempt to answer this complex and painful question. We will begin by looking at influence and mind control in a general sense; we will then examine Christian Science in light of what we know about these issues. As with the discussion of Mrs. Eddy, I will frequently allow the Christian Scientists to speak for themselves in the form of quotations. After all, it should be their words, not mine, which ultimately answer the question at hand.

Notes

1   Daisette D. S. McKenzie, "The Writings of Mary Baker Eddy," *We Know Mary Baker Eddy,* 1st series (Boston: The Christian Science Publishing Society, 1943), 40.

2 Bliss Knapp, "Impressions of Our Leader," *We Knew Mary Baker Eddy*, 1st series (Boston: The Christian Science Publishing Society, 1943), 63.

3 Daisette D. S. McKenzie, *We Knew Mary Baker Eddy*, 1st series, 40-41.

4 Mary Baker Eddy, *Miscellaneous Writings 1883-1896* (Boston: Published by the Trustees under the Will of Mary Baker G. Eddy, 1924), 105:20-23.

5 Richard A. Nenneman, *Persistent Pilgrim: The Life of Mary Baker Eddy* (NH: Nebbadoon Press, 1997), 15.

6 Ibid., 16-18.

7 Willa Cather and Georgine Milmine, *The Life of Mary Baker G. Eddy & the History of Christian Science* (1909; reprint, Lincoln: University of Nebraska Press, 1993), 12-13.

8 Richard A. Nenneman, *Persistent Pilgrim: The Life of Mary Baker Eddy*, 19.

9 Robert Peel, *Mary Baker Eddy: The Years of Discovery* (New York: Holt, Rinehart and Winston, 1966), 22.

10 Richard A. Nenneman, *Persistent Pilgrim: The Life of Mary Baker Eddy*, 52.

11 Willa Cather and Georgine Milmine, *The Life of Mary Baker G. Eddy & the History of Christian Science*: 26, 27.

12 Ibid., 453.

13 Richard A. Nenneman, *Persistent Pilgrim: The Life of Mary Baker Eddy*, 70.

14 Ibid., 82.

15 Ibid., 83.

16 Yvonne Caché von Fettweis and Robert Townsend Warneck, *Mary Baker Eddy: Christian Healer* (Boston: The Christian Science Publishing Society, 1998), xiii, 33-35.

17 Mary Baker Eddy, *Retrospection and Introspection* (Boston: Published by the Trustees under the Will of Mary Baker G. Eddy, 1920), 24: 14-16.

18 Ibid., 24-29.

19 Richard A. Nenneman, *Persistent Pilgrim: The Life of Mary Baker Eddy*, 86-88.

20 Adam Dickey, *Memoirs of Mary Baker Eddy* (1927; reprint, Santa Clarita, CA: The Bookmark, n.d.), vii.

21 Daisette D. S. McKenzie, *We Knew Mary Baker Eddy*, 1st series, 41.

22 Lulu Blackman, "The Star in My Crown of Rejoicing—The Class of 1885," *We Knew Mary Baker Eddy*, 2nd series (Boston: The Christian Science Publishing Society, 1950), 19.

23 Calvin C. Hill, "Some Precious Memories of Mary Baker Eddy," *We Knew Mary Baker Eddy*, 3rd series (Boston: The Christian Science Publishing Society, 1953), 20.

24 Emma C. Shipman, "Mrs. Eddy and the Class of 1898," *We Knew Mary Baker Eddy*, 1st series (Boston: The Christian Science Publishing Society, 1943), 80.

25 Calvin C. Hill, *We Knew Mary Baker Eddy*, 3rd series, 7, and Annie M. Knott, "Reminiscences of Mary Baker Eddy," *We Knew Mary Baker Eddy*, 3rd series (Boston: The Christian Science Publishing Society, 1953), 62.

26 Marion Pinckney Hatch, "Pleasant View," *The Christian Science Journal* 16:4 (1898), 256.

27 Annie Louise Robertson, "The Discoverer and Founder of Christian Science," *We Knew Mary Baker Eddy*, 1st series (Boston: The Christian Science Publishing Society, 1943): 9, and Calvin C. Hill, *We Knew Mary Baker Eddy*, 3rd series, 41.

28   Sue Harper Mims, "An Intimate Picture of Our Leader's Final Class," *We Knew Mary Baker Eddy,* 2nd series (Boston: The Christian Science Publishing Society, 1950), 42.

29   Frank Walter Gale, "Our Leader as Teacher and Friend," *We Knew Mary Baker Eddy,* 2nd series (Boston: The Christian Science Publishing Society, 1950), 23.

30   Annie Louise Robertson, *We Knew Mary Baker Eddy,* 1st series, 9, and Abigail Dyer Thompson, "Loved Memories of Mary Baker Eddy," *We Knew Mary Baker Eddy,* 1st series (Boston: The Christian Science Publishing Society, 1943), 66.

31   Annie M. Knott, *We Knew Mary Baker Eddy,* 3rd series, 61.

32   Emma C. Shipman, *We Knew Mary Baker Eddy,* 1st series, 80.

33   Clara Knox McKee, "With sandals on and staff in hand," *We Knew Mary Baker Eddy,* 2nd series (Boston: The Christian Science Publishing Society, 1950), 73, and Abigail Dyer Thompson, *We Knew Mary Baker Eddy,* 1st series, 68.

34   Yvonne Caché von Fettweis and Robert Townsend Warneck, *Mary Baker Eddy: Christian Healer,* 130.

35   Calvin C. Hill, *We Knew Mary Baker Eddy,* 3rd series, 39.

36   Richard A. Nenneman, *Persistent Pilgrim: The Life of Mary Baker Eddy,* 179.

37   Ibid., 186.

38   Ibid., 152; Yvonne Caché von Fettweis and Robert Townsend Warneck, *Mary Baker Eddy: Christian Healer,* 100.

39   Willa Cather and Georgine Milmine, *The Life of Mary Baker Eddy & the History of Christian Science,* 64-65.

40   Willa Cather and Georgine Milmine, *The Life of Mary Baker Eddy & the History of Christian Science,* 122-123.

41   Mary Baker Eddy, *Message to The Mother Church, Boston, Massachusetts, June, 1901* (Boston: Published by the Trustees under the Will of Mary Baker G. Eddy, 1929), 34:25-26; Mary Baker Eddy, *Message to the First Church of Christ, Scientist or The Mother Church, Boston, June 15, 1902* (Boston, published under the will of Mary Baker G. Eddy, 1930), 4:3-4.

42   Adam H. Dickey, *Memoirs of Mary Baker Eddy,* 43, 44.

43   Richard A. Nenneman, *Persistent Pilgrim: The Life of Mary Baker Eddy,* 156.

44   Adam H. Dickey, *Memoirs of Mary Baker Eddy,* 32.

45   Ibid., 43.

46   Richard A. Nenneman, *Persistent Pilgrim: The Life of Mary Baker Eddy,* 203.

47   Annie Louise Robertson, *We Knew Mary Baker Eddy,* 1st series, 5.

48   Julia Bartlett, "A Worker in the Massachusetts Metaphysical College," *We Knew Mary Baker Eddy,* 4th series (Boston: The Christian Science Publishing Society, 1972), 66-67.

49   Annie M. Knott, *We Knew Mary Baker Eddy,* 3rd series, 69-70.

50   Willa Cather and Georgine Milmine, *The Life of Mary Baker Eddy & the History of Christian Science,* 407.

51   Mary Stewart, "An Interview with Mary Baker Eddy, and Other Memories," *We Knew Mary Baker Eddy,* 2nd series (Boston: The Christian Science Publishing Society, 1950), 60.

52 Emma C. Shipman, *We Knew Mary Baker Eddy,* 1st series, 77.

53 Willa Cather and Georgine Milmine, *The Life of Mary Baker Eddy & the History of Christian Science,* 406-407.

54 Ibid., 406.

55 Ibid., 234.

56 Ibid., 395.

57 For example, Nenneman describes a "hothouse environment" just before the mass defection of 1881 (Richard A. Nenneman, *Persistent Pilgrim,* 151).

58 Adam H. Dickey, *Memoirs of Mary Baker Eddy,* 23.

59 Calvin C. Hill, *We Knew Mary Baker Eddy,* 3rd series, 10-12.

60 Ibid., 39.

61 Willa Cather and Georgine Milmine, *The Life of Mary Baker Eddy & the History of Christian Science,* 232.

62 Ibid., 382.

63 Adam H. Dickey, *Memoirs of Mary Baker Eddy,* 16-17; Martha W. Wilcox, "A Worker in Mrs. Eddy's Chestnut Hill House," *We Knew Mary Baker Eddy,* 4th series (Boston: The Christian Science Publishing Society, 1972), 98.

64 Robert Peel, *Mary Baker Eddy: The Years of Trial,* (New York: Holt, Rinehart & Winston, 1971), 113-115.

65 Adam H. Dickey, *Memoirs of Mary Baker Eddy,* 47-49; Martha Wilcox, *We Knew Mary Baker Eddy,* 4th series, 99-100.

66 Robert Peel, *Mary Baker Eddy: The Years of Trial,* 70.

67 Ibid., 96.

68 Richard A. Nenneman, *Persistent Pilgrim: The Life of Mary Baker Eddy,* 340.

69 Ibid., 338-344.

70 Ibid., 344.

71 Bliss Knapp, *The Destiny of The Mother Church* (1947; reprint, Boston: The Christian Science Publishing Society, 1991).

72 Richard N. Ostling, "Tumult in the Reading Rooms," *Time,* 14 October 1991, 57.

73 Mary Baker Eddy, *Science and Health with Key to the Scriptures* (Boston: Published by the Trustees under the Will of Mary Baker G. Eddy, 1934), 587:5-8.

74 Mary Baker Eddy, *Science and Health,* 591:5-7.

75 Yvonne Caché von Fettweis and Robert Townsend Warneck, *Mary Baker Eddy: Christian Healer,* 188-189.

76 Ibid., 36.

77 "Mrs. Eddy's Place" was published in the 5 June 1943 and 17 November 1962 editions of the *Christian Science Sentinel* and in the July, 1943 and December, 1962 editions of the *Christian Science Journal.* During the 1970s it was also offered as a pamphlet.

78 Mary Stewart, *We Know Mary Baker Eddy,* 2nd series, 64.

79 Judge Septimus J. Hanna and Camilla Hanna, *Reminiscences of Mary Baker Eddy* (reprint, Santa Clarita, CA: The Bookmark, n.d.), 50.

80 Ibid., 51.

81 Ibid., 56.

82 Richard A. Nenneman, *Persistent Pilgrim: The Life of Mary Baker Eddy*, 279.

83 Bliss Knapp, *The Destiny of The Mother Church*, 58.

84 Bliss Knapp, *The Destiny of The Mother Church*, 59.

85 Richard A. Nenneman, *Persistent Pilgrim: The Life of Mary Baker Eddy*, 279.

86 Ibid., 280, 281.

87 Mary Baker Eddy, *Science and Health*, 473:10-17.

88 James Strong, *The Exhaustive Concordance of the Bible* (Iowa Falls, Iowa: World Bible Publishers).

89 Yvonne Caché von Fettweis and Robert Townsend Warneck, *Mary Baker Eddy: Christian Healer*, 4.

90 Ibid., 154.

91 Adam H. Dickey, *Memoirs of Mary Baker Eddy*, 17, 45.

92 Mary Baker Eddy, *Science and Health*, 29:16, 29:32-30:1.

93 Mary Baker Eddy, *Retrospection and Introspection*, (Boston: Published by the Trustees under the Will of Mary Baker G. Eddy, 1920), 70:20-22.

94 Ibid., 70:14-19.

95 *The Christian Science Journal*, vol. 6, November 1888, 402-403.

96 Richard A. Nenneman, *Persistent Pilgrim: The Life of Mary Baker Eddy*, 152, 153.

97 Yvonne Caché von Fettweis and Robert Townsend Warneck, *Mary Baker Eddy: Christian Healer*, 100.

CHAPTER FIVE
Influence and Mind Control

Influence

Everyone is exposed to influence. This is not news to anyone who watches television, reads the newspaper, or tries to debate with a teenager. Communication is full of influence factors designed to change our opinions and to make us act in certain ways. We often yield to influence either consciously or unconsciously. Sometimes our compliance hurts us and at other times it benefits us.

Our susceptibility to influence is not weakness, but a sign of our humanity. It is normal to want to trust others and to find ourselves more susceptible to influence during times of need. Instead of becoming embarrassed when we are duped, it is more productive to learn how influence "works" and how to recognize whether it is being used for our benefit or to our detriment.

Cialdini's Influence Factors

Dr. Robert Cialdini (a self-proclaimed "sucker") conducted a study of the factors that influence society. After extensive research he identified six astonishingly obvious and essentially universal factors that a person can use to "get his way." He discusses these influence techniques in a fascinating book, *Influence: Science and Practice.*[1] Briefly, the factors which influence people the most include:

1. Reciprocation (the law of give and take): We are taught as children to share. If someone gives us something we tend to feel that we somehow "owe" them something in return. For example, if you send me a Christmas card, I feel obligated to send one back to you. This rule also involves the asking of favors. If a very large favor is asked and then reduced to a more reasonable level, compliance with the lesser demand is very high. Babysitting your child for an afternoon doesn't seem so difficult compared to taking all three children for the weekend.

2. Scarcity: Items that are abundantly available are generally considered less valuable than when they are scarce. Having the information that something is about to become scarce makes it even more valuable.

3. Authority: People tend to trust the word of an "expert" simply because he or she is an authority figure. We usually demand less proof from authority figures than from others of "lower" position. This is true even if the "expert" did not really earn the right to be an authority on the subject in question. For example, consider television news casting. We tend to believe what the newscaster says and to assign to him or her a special wisdom, even though newscasters are simply reading what they are told to say. Their look of authority is produced by the way they are dressed, seated, "made-up," and by the well phrased sentences they say without looking as if they are reading them. They tend to gain our trust as we watch them night after night, and the words of newscasters shape and sway public opinion.

4. Consistency: People become more comfortable with an idea once they have made some form of investment in it. An effective way to gain compliance is to begin by asking a very small favor. Once a person is committed to the favor, he or she will likely consent to a slightly larger request. By slowly and systematically raising the requests, the person can be coerced into a large commitment.

5. Social Proof (Consensus): People are more likely to do something if "everybody else" is doing it. This is especially true in situations where the best course of action is unclear.
6. Liking: We are influenced by the people we know and like. Among other factors, we tend to like people when their interests are similar to ours, when we share repeated and positive experiences with them, and when they are physically attractive.

Dr. Cialdini found that compliance is highest when a request is made in an appropriate and pre-arranged context. That is why organizations frequently describe some heartbreaking need or send you a token gift along with their request for financial support.

The influence factors described above can be used in a constructive manner or with selfish motives. What is important to this discussion is how common these factors are and how easy it is to fall prey to them if we are not alert. Once we recognize how easily we can be influenced, we are equipped to ask ourselves questions like, "do I really want to do this?" or "does this make sense?" before we respond to a request or believe what is being said to us.

Cialdini makes it very clear that, once we understand these influence factors, we should use them in an ethical manner. He also points out that unethical influence may work at first but that it often backfires when people stop trusting the perpetrator.

Mind Control

What is mind control (or, more technically, thought reform)? Very simply, it is an extreme form of influence which undermines a person's ability to make informed, independent choices. Mind control plays upon our natural susceptibility to influence as described by Cialdini's model. Victims of thought reform think and act in ways that would seem irrational or immoral to them if they were not being controlled. People fall prey to mind control when they become involved with a person, group, or ideology which influences them to the point that their own attitudes and actions are superseded by those of the controlling person(s) or ideology. The victim develops what is called a "pseudo identity" which masks, but does not destroy, his or her own personality. The important distinction between mind control and a conscious change of attitude is that the victim of mind control is not aware that it is occurring. It happens subtly and a piece at a time.[2]

Under the influence of a pseudo-identity the victim thinks, does, and says things that he/she would otherwise consider to be crazy or even abhorrent. This is what happens to people who become trapped in cults. It explains why otherwise moral people are willing to misuse their bodies, steal, lie, eat garbage and do all kinds of things that horrify them when they finally break free from the cult. It also explains why the friends and families of cult victims make comments like "when I saw her she was like a completely different person. I didn't know her anymore."

People do not yield to mind control deliberately. They usually become ensnared during a time of insecurity, loneliness, or crisis. They may be in a period of transition, such as changing jobs or attending college for the first time. Perhaps they are struggling with poor health or have just lost an important relationship. Whatever the issue, someone steps in, offers comfort, and begins to provide what is lacking. The person, group, or ideology seems wonderful at first—full of loving support, meaning, purpose, and fulfillment. As the victim becomes more deeply involved with the group, he begins to conform a little at a time, adopting the group's lingo and cultural style while trying to "fit in." Little by little the victim loses touch with his former "self" as he responds to the rewards, discipline, and new ideas that gradually engulf him. Finally, he becomes dependent upon the group or ideology and somehow unable to function without them, even if they have become abusive. The group has convinced him that he is not good enough to make it without them, that the rest of the world is somehow "bad" or inferior, or that something terrible will happen to him if he leaves.

I have just described the basic workings of a cult, a gang, or any group that uses deceptive tactics to maintain control over its members. Members of these groups sometimes live in communes and dress strangely; they often look and act normal, hold regular jobs, and function within society. They may live on your block or even in your family.

During the 1940s and 1950s, Robert J. Lifton studied the thought reform techniques used in Chinese prison camps and at Chinese universities. In this study, he showed that mind control does not have to be overtly forced upon a person. The prisoners were obviously under duress, but the students were attending their universities by choice. Both groups fell victim to the government's mind control program. Lifton used the Chinese study to identify eight criteria present in a thought reform program.[3] These criteria were later found applicable to high demand and cult groups in general. A group may not use all of the criteria to control its followers, but the degree to which Lifton's criteria are present is usually a good indicator of how controlling or "cultic" the group is. Questionable groups are often evaluated against Lifton's criteria in order to determine whether they exercise undue control over their members.

It should be noted that, except for the cult leader, the upper echelon of mind-controlling groups is not necessarily composed of bad or selfish people. These people are usually as brainwashed as their subordinates and really believe that they are doing the right thing as they perpetuate the rules and practices of their group. Ironically, even the cult leader may be self- deceived or mentally unbalanced and may actually believe that he or she is behaving appropriately.

Lifton's Eight Criteria for Thought Reform

1. Milieu Control—Milieu control involves information management. It typically includes the control of what a person reads, hears, discusses, thinks, etc. It may involve removing a person from his or her environment or simply keeping the individual busy in activities, meditation, reading the group's material, or with other activities that reduce the amount of time available for interaction with outsiders.
2. Mystical Manipulation—Mystical manipulation involves a leader's claim to divine or spiritual authority, allowing the leader to interpret events as he or she wishes. It enables a leader to make prophecies

and to interpret everyday events as signs and wonders which validate the group ideology. These interpretations create certain emotions and behaviors which are contrived, but which have a mystical quality about them and seem to arise spontaneously from within the group. Mystical manipulation is easier when the group members' critical thinking skills have been dulled by fatigue, poor nutrition, too much activity, and the like.

3. The Demand for Purity—The world is divided into good and bad, black and white. Members must continually strive to achieve humanly unattainable purity. This impossible task inevitably produces feelings of guilt and failure.

4. The Cult of Confession—There is usually an over-emphasis on confession, either to individuals or to the entire group. While confession is not bad in itself, its overemphasis places members in a vulnerable position as their weaknesses are exposed and are often used against them.

5. The Sacred Science—The group has various doctrines and teachings which comprise what is called its "sacred science." The beliefs and teachings are considered sacred because they are supposedly from an indisputable source such as divine revelation or inspiration. They are a science because they are precise and able to explain everything. Both the sacred science and the leader who touts it are above criticism.

6. Loading the Language—The group has its own jargon which supports the sacred science. The jargon changes the meanings of common words so that members are unable to effectively communicate with people outside the group. This "loaded language" includes thought-stopping clichés which hinder the members' ability to think clearly about the issues at hand. For example, outsiders may be labeled as "the unenlightened" or as "instruments of Satan." A member is less likely to believe criticism of his or her group from someone whom he or she automatically thinks of as unenlightened or evil.

7. Doctrine Over Person—The group's doctrine is more important than the individual. Experiences contradicting the doctrine must be ignored or reinterpreted. In matters of disagreement between

the doctrine and the individual's beliefs or experience, the doctrine and group teachings are always right and the individual is always wrong.

8. Dispensing of Existence—The group claims the authority to decide who has the right to exist and who does not. This is usually taken figuratively but means that the group considers non-members to be unspiritual, damned, evil, and the like. Occasionally a group decides that it has the right to kill outsiders. In any case, this elitist attitude often results in the shunning of members who choose to leave the group. It also helps to create a fear of leaving, because to leave results in damnation, failure, or some other disaster.

Christian Science and Mind Control

Does Christian Science involve mind control? I sometimes find myself thinking, "Most Christian Scientists are friendly, independent, intellectual, successful people. They are not told how to dress, what to eat, and how to run their lives. Their churches are loosely-knit and their members usually have more contact with outsiders than with each other. How could these people be victims of mind control?" Then I remember life as a Christian Scientist—living in the material world while trying to demonstrate its non-existence; suffering needlessly while trying to heal medically-treatable ailments; watching people die for reasons which were rarely explained and knowing that it was unacceptable to probe for answers; suffering (or watching others suffer) quietly because to talk about a problem was to "give it reality;" and being taught that leaving Christian Science would make me susceptible to illness and other problems that befall those who step out from under the Christian Science umbrella.

My Christian Science friends and I were not openly forced into our beliefs and practices; we were offered utopian promises that kept us striving to live up to the standards of our religion so we could reap its benefits. All we had to do was study Mary Baker Eddy's writings, understand them, and put them into practice.

Understanding and applying the principles of Christian Science would give us dominion over the (seeming) problems we faced in this (seeming) material existence. If we failed in one instance, we just had to study harder. Our failure was not due to our religion but to our own lack of understanding. The system was always right. We just had to understand it better—to try harder. Most of the controls that molded our thought patterns were not openly imposed upon us but were quietly implanted through our religion's doctrine. Promises of healing, "salvation" from material limitations, a sense of spiritual superiority, and the knowledge that believing in materiality was dangerous—these enticements and "knowledge" kept us striving to understand the "ultimate truth" of Christian Science; they molded our thoughts and the way we ran our lives.

Those of us who have left Christian Science are surprised by what we believed and tolerated while under Mrs. Eddy's influence. Some of us have been able to shake off the experience with few ill effects; others have suffered emotional fallout for years. As we discuss our experiences in Christian Science, we are amazed by what we believed and how we and/or our families dealt with the normal challenges of life. It is clear to us that we were trapped within a closed system of circular logic.

As a Christian Scientist, I used to grow tired of non-Scientists telling me about some Christian Scientist they knew who had died. My Christian Science friends and I would attribute these stories to flukes, sensationalism, and to the spiritual failures and poor judgment of the person who had died. "Of course you shouldn't die in Christian Science," we would say. "If you can't handle the problem, call a doctor!" But was this a fair statement for us to make in a religion that encourages "radical reliance" on Christian Science, applauds the seemingly hopeless cases where people did NOT call the doctor and were healed when all seemed lost, and teaches that relying on medicine will damage one's spiritual progress? When we *did* rely on medicine, didn't we feel that we had to keep quiet about it?

After I left Christian Science, I began to think back on all of those "so-and-so died" stories and to remember the tragedies I witnessed while a Christian Scientist. Then I met a number of former Christian Scientists and heard their stories, some of which were truly gruesome. I started to realize that I was hearing too many of these stories and being told of too many emotional problems for them to represent flukes and sensationalism. I thought of how few fresh testimonies I had heard during the Wednesday night testimony meetings (many people described healings which had happened long ago). I began to realize that something is terribly wrong in this religion which teaches that sin, disease, and death are unreal while promising a reliable, "scientific system" of healing to all who wholeheartedly follow its teachings.

The Christian Science Church has "documented" many healings (the term "documented" must be used loosely since most "healings" involve problems which have never been medically diagnosed). These "healings" fall into many categories which may or may not actually be the result of Christian Science treatment. Some "healings" are simply the result of the body's own natural processes. Others represent the relief of stress-related or misdiagnosed symptoms. Some can only be explained from a Christian or Satanic perspective.[4] What is NOT well documented are the huge number of unhealed cases, the unexplained deaths, and the denied problems which finally either go away or permanently maim the patient. What is also largely ignored is the huge psychological toll I have observed in this religion: good, solid Christian Science families that end up with emotionally confused, angry, or troubled children. Finally, what is unreported are the secret trips to the doctor which create a sense of guilt and failure within this religion of seeming health and rose-colored glasses.

In trying to understand the discrepancy between what Christian Science promises and the harm it causes to so many of its followers, I decided to examine the religion against a mind control model. I chose Lifton's model because it represents the classic study on the subject. The following discussion will cover each of Lifton's criteria except for "the cult of confession" (Christian Science involves affirmation of one's perfection more than open confession of one's faults). To the Christian Scientist I say, "Don't be afraid to look. If I am wrong you have nothing to worry about." To the former Christian Scientist I say, "This exercise might be painful, but perhaps it will answer some of your nagging questions.

Perhaps it will 'put some of the puzzle pieces together,' as it has done for many with whom I have shared."

Notes

1 Robert B. Cialdini, *Influence: Science and Practice, second edition* (Arizona State University: HarperCollins Publishers, 1988).

2 For more information about cults and mind control, see: Margaret Thaler Singer with Janja Lalich, *Cults in Our Midst: The Hidden Menace in our Everyday Lives* (San Francisco: Jossey-Bass Publishers, 1995); Steven Hassan, *Combating Cult Mind Control* (Rochester, VT: Park Street Press, 1988); Paul R. Martin, *Cult Proofing Your Kids* (Grand Rapids, MI: Zondervan Publishing House, 1993).

3 Robert Jay Lifton, *Thought Reform and the Psychology of Totalism: A Study of "Brainwashing" in China* (Chapel Hill: The University of North Carolina Press, 1989), Chapter 22.

4 For examples of Satanic influence in miracles and healing, see Exod. 7:10-11, 20-22; Exod. 8:6-7; 2 Cor. 11:13-15; 2 Thess. 2:8-9; and Rev. 13:11-14, 16:14.

CHAPTER SIX
Milieu Control-What Can We Know?

Milieu control involves the control of information. It deals not only with outside influences such as what a person hears and reads, but also with what he is allowed to think and say. These controls isolate a person from his former reference points and from outside opinions which might make him question the doctrine or actions of those who are controlling him.

Christian Science is replete with information controls. Consider the following examples:

Literature—When studying the subject of spiritual healing, Christian Scientists are instructed to read only Church-approved literature. *The Manual of The Mother Church* states:

The Bible, together with *Science and Health* and other works by Mrs. Eddy, shall be his only textbooks for self-instruction in Christian Science, and for teaching and practicing metaphysical healing.[1]

Notice that metaphysical healing is generalized here, invalidating any method but Christian Science. *The Manual* also states:

> It shall be the privilege and duty of every member, who can afford it, to subscribe for the periodicals which are organs of this Church; and it shall be the duty of the Directors to see that these periodicals are ably edited and kept abreast of the times.[2]

The Mother Church (specifically, the Board of Directors, working through the Christian Science Publishing Society) decides which spiritual information its membership should read and which information it should not read (although there is no official policing of what members read). This control may seem reasonable to Mrs. Eddy's followers since it protects her "divinely inspired" doctrine from contamination by mere human opinion. Its effect, however, is to limit a believer's opportunity to evaluate Mrs. Eddy's ideas against outside information.

While attending Principia College, a school for Christian Scientists, I took a course that taught the religion's history. As we studied Christian Science and its leader, we learned which biographies of Mrs. Eddy were "trustworthy" and which were "inaccurate." I recently reviewed my notes and was intrigued by how much of the class focused on discrediting the "inaccurate" biographies. I still struggle a bit with those "good" and "bad" labels when I approach material on Christian Science. I have finally read some of the taboo writings and have found that many of the apparent discrepancies between the "good" and "bad" literature lie not in the facts regarding Christian Science and its history, but in the interpretation of those facts. Now, instead of simply discounting the unapproved ("unauthorized") material, I look for hints within the authorized literature which either support or refute the unauthorized writings. I think this is a healthier approach than simply following The Mother Church's decision regarding what I should or should not read.

Despite the by-laws stated above, it is unclear how Mrs. Eddy really felt about reputable Christian Scientists publishing outside the Publishing Society's direct authority. Whether or not her attitude changed in later years, she made the following statement in the July 1891 edition of *The Christian Science Journal*: "I consider my students as capable, individually, of selecting their own reading material and circulating it, as a committee would be which is chosen for this purpose." This statement seems to discourage the concept of "authorized" literature, although, from her ever-tightening controls in later years, I question whether she would have made this statement in 1910.

Whatever Mrs. Eddy's final attitude regarding the subject of authorization, the fact remains that The Mother Church has been controlling the flow of information since the early 1900s. It suppressed Adam Dickey's memoirs shortly after his wife published them in 1927, even though Mrs. Eddy had asked him to write the memoirs.[3] The Church has also suppressed the publication of many other doctrinal and historical works throughout the years. Unflattering works like (Cather and) Milmine's 1909 biography have disappeared rather quickly after their publication.[4]

The Cather/Milmine biography provides an example of the Church's quiet attempts to silence opposition. When, in 1907, McClure's Magazine began publishing the biography in serial form, three Church representatives visited the magazine office and tried to suppress the story. After the series was published as a book, Christian Scientists apparently purchased and destroyed most of the books and interfered with the availability of library copies by constantly checking them out. Someone sympathetic to Christian Science bought the book's copyright. The book's printing plates were subsequently destroyed and its manuscripts ended up in the Archives and Library of The Mother Church.[5]

Edwin Dakin's biography, *Mrs. Eddy,* was also suppressed by the Church after its publication in 1929. The editor's note in the 1930 edition describes how, after the book received a number of favorable reviews, the Christian Scientists launched a "virulent . . . campaign for [its] suppression." Bookstores were intimidated to the point that many stopped selling the books or kept them hidden. According to the editor's note, assuring the book's availability became an issue not of economics, but of "freedom of the mind." Freedom finally prevailed as book suppliers and the public recognized the attempted censorship and rallied against it. According to the publisher, the success of Dakin's book represents "the failure of an organized Minority to accomplish the suppression of opinions not to its liking."[6]

Ann Beals' experience provides a recent example of how the Church has continued to oppose unauthorized literature. Beals was a practitioner listed in *The Christian Science Journal* who also wrote metaphysical articles for both the *Christian Science Monitor* and Christian Science periodicals. As she observed the general decline in church membership and the need for more effective healing, she became convinced that the Christian Science movement could be strengthened if "more advanced" writings on Christian Science would be published and freely circulated. She discussed the matter with officials at The Mother Church but discovered that they were not interested in her idea. In 1974,

> . . . she wrote and published independently of the Church her booklet, *Animal Magnetism*. She did this in defiance of the Church policy of "authorized literature" which prohibits members from publishing, circulating, or reading any literature on Christian Science not published or approved by the Church. Within a few months she was forced to resign her listing [as a practitioner] in the *Journal,* and the editors of the periodicals would no longer accept her articles.[7]

Beals was not dissuaded by the Church's policy of censorship. She founded The Bookmark, a bookstore which publishes and sells Christian Science literature suppressed by the Church. These publications include works by members of Mrs. Eddy's "inner circle," lectures by Church-authorized lecturers, and writings by a growing number of brave souls who are no longer afraid to defy the Church's authorization policy. Beals claims that writings offered through The Bookmark "conform strictly to the teachings of Mary Baker Eddy."[8]

Church services—The control continues in church services. Christian Science churches have no pastors or official leaders. The "sermon" for each week consists of readings from the Bible and *Science and Health*. The readings are compiled by a secret committee at The Mother Church and are based on a set of rotating topics dictated by Mrs. Eddy. These "Lesson-Sermons" are published, in advance, in a booklet called the *Christian Science Quarterly*. Members study the week's Lesson-Sermon every day during the week; it is then read from the pulpit on Sunday by two Readers previously elected by the congregation. These Readers are not allowed to comment on what they read or to offer any independent input, except that the First Reader selects the music and two short Bible passages to read at the beginning and end of the service. As a result, Christian Science services are virtually identical all over the world.

Wednesday night "Testimony Meetings" allow the First Reader a little more freedom as he or she makes up a set of readings on any topic of his or her choice. These readings, however, are still taken exclusively from *Science and Health* and the Bible. Again, the reader is not permitted to make any personal comments about the message.

The testimony meetings allow time for Christian Scientists to tell others how they have been healed using Christian Science. The *Manual* states, however, that they may not include any discussion of suffering or symptoms, although they may include the generic name of the disease that was healed.[9] These rules also apply to testimonies given in the Christian Science periodicals.

Lectures—The Church maintains a special group of lecturers who travel the country giving talks on various topics related to Christian Science. The content of these lectures must be approved by the Church.

Special Training—Serious students of Christian Science usually take a two-week course called "class instruction." The course is taught by a Church-trained and approved teacher. Teachers use only the Bible and Mrs. Eddy's writings and are not allowed to interject any personal views into the curriculum.[10]

These controls are not inherently bad since their purpose is to maintain the purity of what Christian Scientists consider to be an exact spiritual science. The problem is that these kinds of controls have resulted in a congregation that questions very little and has placed far too much trust in its leadership. This trust has made the people open to other, more serious controls. Many of these controls involve the actual process of healing and the constraints placed upon members who struggle with healing. They will be discussed in the chapters addressing "mystical manipulation," "doctrine over person," and "the demand for purity."

The most dangerous form of Christian Science milieu control involves the filtering of reality. A Christian Scientist lives in an almost constant state of denial as he or she filters out the material elements of the world and replaces them with spiritual interpretations. The Christian Scientist is taught that matter is unreal—the material world is an illusion and physical senses cannot be trusted. To grow spiritually and obtain healings, the individual must reinterpret events so that they mesh with his or her spiritualized world view. For example, if a woman injures her hand, she must not try to heal a physical hand. She must "understand" that she is a purely spiritual reflection of God and cannot, therefore, be injured. To put it bluntly, she must know that she does not even have a physical hand to be injured.

The average Christian Scientist may sound perfectly normal when discussing various aspects of the material world with "Science" or "non-Science" friends. The person is, however, living a dual reality—functioning within the material illusion "on the outside," while simultaneously spiritualizing and denying these material elements in the mind. For example, I can remember many conversations in which someone would tell me of an illness and I would listen and respond with "oh, that's too bad," and other appropriate remarks. At the same time I was making these statements I was mentally declaring that the illness was not real. I remember feeling as though I was straddling two different worlds. In a way, I *was* living in two different realities with no good way to evaluate either one of them.

It is interesting to examine some of Mrs. Eddy's statements regarding the spiritual and material states of existence (a Christian Scientist would call them the "Absolute" and the "Relative"). In her autobiography, Mrs. Eddy states,

> It is well to know, dear reader, that our material, mortal history is but the record of dreams, not of man's real existence, and the dream has no place in the Science of being. It is "as a tale that is told," and "as the shadow when it declineth." The heavenly intent of earth's shadows is to chasten the affections, to rebuke human consciousness and turn it gladly from a material, false sense of life and happiness, to spiritual joy and true estimate of being. . . . Mere historic incidents and personal events are frivolous and of no moment, unless they illustrate the ethics of Truth. To this end, but only to this end, such narrations may be admissible and advisable; but if spiritual conclusions are separated from their premises, the [connection] is lost, and the argument, with its rightful conclusions, becomes correspondingly obscure. The human history needs to be revised, and the material record expunged.[11]

While discussing the value of disregarding spurious evidence in a scientific experiment, a Christian Science chemist quotes Mrs. Eddy as saying,

> Erroneous belief is destroyed by truth. Change the evidence, and that disappears which before seemed real to this false belief, and the human consciousness rises higher.[12]

Notice the difference here between disregarding evidence which is not pertinent to a problem and *changing* evidence as suggested by Mrs. Eddy. Evidence can be disregarded, but by its nature it cannot be altered. What is, is. Mrs. Eddy teaches her students not only to disregard reality, but also to somehow change it.

Mrs. Eddy made some other interesting comments about replacing material existence with a spiritualized interpretation of reality. When a clergyman asked to visit her she responded,

> Should I give myself the pleasant pastime of seeing your personal self, or give you the opportunity of seeing mine, you would not see me thus, for I am not there. I have risen to look and wait and watch and pray for the spirit of Truth that leadeth away from person—from body to Soul, even to the true image and likeness of God.[13]

In another classic illustration of Christian Science logic, Mrs. Eddy wrote to a student, "I have just found what did (but did not) produce a temporary tempest here."[14] By this logic, a person *is,* but *is not* sick, hurt, or any other material condition. The material dream says that the person is experiencing the problem, but spiritual reality says that he or she is not.

Is not this constant reinterpretation of reality the ultimate milieu control? It emotionally separates the Christian Scientist from himself and from society, yet it requires no fences, fatigue, or other controls often maintained in mind control environments. All it needs is the promise of healing and perfection.

Notes

1 Mary Baker Eddy, *Manual of The Mother Church,* 89th ed., Article IV.

2 Ibid., Article VIII, SEC. 14.

3 Adam H. Dickey, *Memoirs of Mary Baker Eddy* (1927; reprint, Santa Clarita, CA: The Bookmark, n.d.), v.

4 *The Life of Mrs. Eddy & the History of Christian Science,* 497-498. This book was originally published with Georgine Milmine as the sole author. It was later realized that Willa Cather probably wrote the biography using Milmine's research.

5 Willa Cather and Georgine Milmine, *The Life of Mary Baker G. Eddy & the History of Christian Science* (1909; reprint, Lincoln: University of Nebraska Press, 1993), 497-498.

6 Edwin Franden Dakin, *Mrs. Eddy: The Biography of a Virginal Mind* (New York: Charles Scribner's Sons, 1930), vi.

7 Catalog for The Bookmark, Fall/Winter 1998, Box. 801143, Santa Clarita, CA 91380, p. 30.

8   Ibid., 30.

9   Mary Baker Eddy, *Manual of The Mother Church,* 89th ed., Article VIII, SEC. 24.

10   Ibid., Article XXVI.

11   Mary Baker Eddy, *Retrospection and Introspection* (Boston: Published by the Trustees under the Will of Mary Baker G. Eddy, 1920), 21:13-20, 21:25-22:2.

12   James Richard Bartels-Keith, "Chemistry and the Christian Scientist," *The Christian Science Journal* 95, (1977): 82. (Science and Health, 297:12-14).

13   Mary Baker Eddy, *The First Church of Christ, Scientist, and Miscellany,* (Boston: Published by the Trustees under the Will of Mary Baker G. Eddy, 1941), 119; also quoted by Calvin C. Hill in *We Knew Mary Baker Eddy,* 3rd series, 21.

14   Willa Cather and Georgine Milmine, *The Life of Mary Baker Eddy & the History of Christian Science,* 394.

CHAPTER SEVEN
Mystical Manipulation

Mystical manipulation involves a leader's claim to spiritual authority. This authority allows the leader to make rules, prophecies, and interpretations which add a mystical or spiritual quality to events experienced or observed by members of his or her group. These manipulated or spiritually interpreted events support the group's ideology and allow the leader to control its members.

"What?" exclaims the Christian Scientist. "You think that Christian Science involves mystical manipulation? Boy, are you confused! Christian Science is founded upon unbiased and spiritually scientific facts. It is not based upon Mrs. Eddy's personal theories, but upon Jesus' teachings and example. The miracles and healings Christian Scientists perform are not mystical or even supernatural; they are 'divinely natural' as they prove what Jesus taught—that sin, disease, and death are unreal because matter is unreal. Mrs. Eddy did not manipulate her students, but simply taught them the Truth as God gave it to her. In fact, she denounced spiritualism, mesmerism, and hypnotism, and wrote that '[Christian] Science never removes phenomena from the domain of reason into the realm of mysticism."[1] She even studied her own writings as a student and objected to her students becoming attached to her personality. Does that sound like one who manipulates her followers?"

"No," I reply to the Christian Scientist. "This description of Mrs. Eddy does not sound like one who would consciously manipulate her followers. But I have looked beneath the surface, studying the historical records and observing the way she dealt with her students. Unfortunately, my search has revealed a strong pattern of manipulation. Am I accusing Mrs. Eddy of intentional dishonesty or sinister motives? No. I believe that her manipulative and authoritarian style was not a conscious attempt to control and hurt people; it was the result of her personality, physical and emotional makeup, and belief system. Nevertheless, Mrs. Eddy's doctrine and leadership style *did* and *still do* involve a tremendous amount of mystical manipulation."

I will begin by listing some events and attitudes which suggest the presence of mystical manipulation. These attitudes will lead us to the sinister and extremely manipulative doctrine of animal magnetism.

- Mrs. Eddy's claim to divine revelation allowed her to create a new definition of reality and describe it with biblical terms that she modified to fit her purposes. This new reality and language form the basis for the healing work demanded by Christian Science and for the explanation of failed healings. These issues will be discussed below and in later chapters.
- Through stories about her childhood, Mrs. Eddy suggested that she was chosen by God to receive His revelation. Dickey recounts several of these tales in his memoirs. Among other interesting items, the stories claim that she had a special ability to heal as a child and that she was audibly called by God.[2] Her story about being called by God is similar to the biblical account of Samuel being called and finally answering, "Speak, Lord; for thy servant heareth."[3] Mrs. Eddy describes this incident in her autobiography, Retrospection and Introspection, but when she told the story to Dickey she added that she was levitated off the

bed three times after she answered the Lord. She told Dickey that she "pondered [the levitation] deeply in her heart and thought of it many years afterward, when she was demonstrating the nothingness of matter and that the claim of the human body was a myth."

- Healings supposedly prove that Christian Science is a valid belief system. Testimonies of healing are therefore highly emphasized. Every church holds Wednesday night testimony meetings and the Church periodicals always tell of healings in the Christian Science community. Every major Christian Science gathering I have attended has had a designated time for testimonies. It is interesting that these testimonies usually end with phrases like "I am very grateful to Christian Science" or "I am very grateful to Mrs. Eddy," but are much less likely to end with "I am very grateful to God for this healing."

- Mrs. Eddy's followers often attributed everyday events in her life to the effects of animal magnetism or mental malpractice (a form of evil which will be explained below). Annie Knott stated that the seventy-one-year-old Mrs. Eddy had white hair because of "the tremendous efforts called for in ascending the mount of revelation"[4] (rather than because of her age). Other workers noted that she often experienced severe physical problems when struggling with important church-related decisions. They attributed her symptoms to the resistance of animal magnetism or the work of mental malpractitioners rather than to the stress many people (myself included) feel when having to make difficult decisions.[5] It is well known that common stress can cause physical symptoms, but this fact was ignored by Mrs. Eddy's followers.

- Mrs. Eddy claimed that her husband Gilbert was mentally murdered—but this cannot be understood without launching into the concept of animal magnetism and mental malpractice.

Animal Magnetism (or, the terrible power of . . . nothing)

Animal magnetism deals with the belief that there is existence, thought, or power apart from God. In Mrs. Eddy's words:

> As named in Christian Science, animal magnetism or hypno-
> tism is the specific term for error, or mortal mind. It is the
> false belief that mind is in matter, and is both evil and good;
> that evil is as real as good and more powerful. This belief has
> not one quality of Truth. It is either ignorant or malicious. The
> malicious form of hypnotism ultimates in moral idiocy. The
> truths of immortal Mind sustain man, and they annihilate the
> fables of mortal mind, whose flimsy and gaudy pretensions,
> like silly moths, singe their own wings and fall into dust.[6]

If animal magnetism is a false belief, and if thoughts and beliefs determine our experience, it follows that thoughts can be used to hurt as well as to
heal. Mrs. Eddy defines the deliberate interference with another's thoughts
and/or health as mental malpractice or malicious animal magnetism.

> All mental malpractice arises from ignorance or malice afore-
> thought. It is the injurious action of one mortal mind control-
> ling another from wrong motives, and it is practiced either
> with a mistaken or a wicked purpose.[7]

The concept of animal magnetism can be complex and confusing.
It, like other concepts related to matter, is considered by the Christian
Scientist to be unreal. It only has the power that we give it. Yet its power
(no, its non-power) plays a major role in the lives of Christian Scientists,
both today and in Mrs. Eddy's day. It is non-existent, yet is described in
anthropomorphic terms and can cause untold destruction in the lives of
the unwary. Mrs. Eddy told the students attending an 1882 meeting of the
Christian Scientist Association that "all there is to mesmerism is what
we make of it."[8] In an 1895 *Christian Science Journal* article she stated,
"Animal magnetism, hypnotism, etc., are disarmed by the practitioner

who excludes from his own consciousness, and that of his patients, all sense of the realism of any other cause or effect save that which cometh from God."[9]

Yet, consider some of the havoc blamed on animal magnetism in Mrs. Eddy's day:

Mr. Eddy's death: Despite an autopsy conclusively showing heart damage, Mrs. Eddy publicly proclaimed that her husband was mentally murdered. She privately blamed a disaffected student named Daniel Arens for administering the "mental arsenic" that killed him.[10]

Negative thoughts about Mrs. Eddy: Students who left Christian Science were thought to be under the mental influence of other disaffected students. The third edition of *Science and Health* railed against Kennedy, Spofford, and Arens as a main source of much malpractice, although this direct personal attack was removed in later editions.

Loyal students who entertained negative thoughts about Mrs. Eddy were also thought to be under mesmeric influence. For example, during the late 1880s Mrs. Eddy listed the Christmas gifts she received each year in the *Christian Science Journal*. Her publisher tried to dissuade her from this practice in 1890, but she sent him the following reply:

> Students are constantly telling me how they felt the *mental* impression this year to make me *no* present, and when they overcame it were strengthened and blessed. For this reason— viz., to discourage mental malpractice and to encourage those who beat it—I want that notice published.[11]

Judge Hanna attended the last class that Mrs. Eddy held—a class to which she invited only a select group of students. He made the following comment during the class and was heartily supported by many others present:

> Mother, let me tell you this. Sometimes all the machinations of evil that are conceivable to the human mind seem to be hurled at us, and sometimes for days the world seems black. Every argument that the ingenuity of evil can suggest whispers, trying

to hide your mission, and the light returns only when we see you as you are—the revelator of this Truth.

Mrs. Eddy responded,

My dear children, if you had not seen it, I should have had to teach you this. I could not have avoided telling you that when my students become blinded to me as the one through whom Truth has come in this age, they miss the path.[12]

Peel describes how Clara Choate wrote to Mrs. Eddy about finding one of the students "mentally drowsy." He continues,

She had told Miss Brooks the cause and cure of her condition (*i.e.*, the aggressive mental suggestions of the malpractitioners, to be recognized and rejected as such) and commented to Mrs. Eddy, "The usual sign 'displeasure of you' was first presented but soon wore off and the more I worked the faster it disappeared."[13]

Direct attacks against Mrs. Eddy: As the leader of a religious movement which would destroy the belief in materiality, Mrs. Eddy and her students believed that she was the primary target for mortal mind's attacks. Her frequent emotional and physical problems were attributed to these attacks, as were any glitches that accompanied the publishing of her writings. Mrs. Eddy's writings, her students' memoirs, and the biographies contain many references to the idea that Mrs. Eddy was the focal point for error's concentrated assault. This belief explains the mental bodyguard she kept in her household. Dickey explains it well:

Many people seemed to be inspired with a belief that there could be no pleasanter occupation in the world than to work for Mrs. Eddy. They failed to realize that what Mrs. Eddy wanted and actually required of those about her was the mental support which she found necessary to receive from students in order that she might be uninterrupted in her work for her Cause and for mankind. Mrs. Eddy was at the head of a great Movement, a Church that had grown up under divine direction and was designed, eventually, to destroy all evil and bring to suffering humanity a remedy for every form of sickness and sin. The same form of evil that attacked the work of Jesus and cried out, "What have we to do with thee, thou Jesus of Nazareth? art thou come to destroy us?" (Mark 1:24) was by no means lacking in connection with Mrs. Eddy's experience. She was in a position somewhat similar to that of the general of a large army, who is fighting for its existence. The attacks of the enemy would be made, if possible, on the leader of the defending army.... She must be in the front rank in the thick of battle every day, and she needed to be surrounded by the best workers she could find, who virtually acted as a bodyguard....[14]

She explained [to Dickey] that as the Leader of a great Movement, she had naturally acquired many enemies, and that she was having considerable to meet by way of aggressive mental suggestion, intended to injure or affect her physically.[15]

The most important work in connection with our Leader's home was done by the mental workers.... This work was done under the direct supervision of our Leader.... Her secretary, at her request, prepared what was denominated a "watch." This consisted of ... the names or description of the phases of error that Mrs. Eddy wished them to handle. She was being constantly assailed by mental malpractice.... She seemed to be the only one who was able to discern the course that error was pursuing.... On one of these occasions, when the suffering seemed severe, she called us all into the room.... It was at this time that she said to us, "You don't any of you realize what is going on. This is a dark hour for the Cause and you do not seem to be awake to it." She said, "I am now working on a plane that would mean instantaneous death to any of you."[16]

Mrs. Eddy had Dickey promise her that, *if* she were to die, he would write his memoirs regarding his time in her household and report that she was mentally murdered (note that she made this request in 1908, two years before her death).[17]

Discord between Christian Scientists: The 1880s was an especially volatile decade for Christian Science as the young movement began to take shape. Many of Mrs. Eddy's students lived with her at the Massachusetts Metaphysical College, which was actually her house at 8 Broad Street in Lynn, Massachusetts. These years were marked by several lawsuits between Mrs. Eddy and disaffected students, by the volatile third edition of *Science and Health* with its attacks on Kennedy, Spofford, and Arens, and by much stress within the ranks of the Metaphysical College itself. Much of the tension revolved around the issue of mental malpractice, both from outside the college and among students within the college. Mrs. Eddy warned her students about malpractice from fellow students, as when she wrote to Clara Choate, "Won't you be careful not to give Mr. Howard occasion to think you malpractice?"[18] Mrs. Eddy could be gentle with her students, but often rebuked them quite harshly. Peel describes one of these rebukes as it related to the subject of malpractice:

> Some of the students were growing restive under her exhortations, but when one of them asked her one day whether she didn't feel that the time had come to say less about animal magnetism, Mrs. Eddy sprang to her feet, struck her hands together, and cried, "Leave me at once."[19]

The biographers suggest that Mrs. Eddy began to depersonalize animal magnetism as the years went on and began to think of it more as a general state of mortal mind instead of always emanating from individuals (although unwary individuals could be used as instruments of animal magnetism). Despite this depersonalization, its importance in Christian Science theology never really waned. This is illustrated by the "watches" described above, which continued essentially until the end of Mrs. Eddy's life. It is further indicated by the comments of Martha Wilcox, who joined Mrs. Eddy's household in 1908. One of the first lessons that Mrs. Eddy gave her was a lesson about mental malpractice. Miss Wilcox made the following comment regarding the lesson: "This lesson on mental malpractice was quite apropos for one entering a household comprised of never less than 17 up to 25 so-called personalities."[20] This is an extremely interesting comment considering the fact that Miss Wilcox was talking about a group of top-notch Christian Scientists, handpicked because of their unusual spirituality and willingness to work together to help their leader. If they needed to guard against each other's thoughts, then heaven help the rest of us.

The weather: Mrs. Eddy blamed animal magnetism for unpleasant weather. She detested thunderstorms and heavy snowfalls as she thought them to be manifestations of error. She appointed members of her household and also a special committee in Boston to deal with the weather on a spiritual level. Her description of their role provides a good illustration of how a Christian Science treatment works:

> A Christian Scientist has no business attempting to control or govern the weather any more than he has a right to attempt to control or govern sickness, but he does know, and must know, that God governs the weather and no other influence can be brought to bear upon it. When we destroy mortal mind's belief that it is a creator, and that it produces all sorts of weather, good as well as bad, we shall then realize God's perfect weather and be the recipients of His bounty in that respect. God's weather is always right. A certain amount of rain and sunshine is natural and normal, and we have no right to interfere with the stately operations of divine wisdom in regulating meteorological conditions. . . . the weather belongs

to God, and when we destroy the operations of mortal mind and leave the question of regulating the weather to God, we shall have weather conditions as they should be.[21]

Dickey continues,

I have heard our Leader describe in a number of instances how she has dissipated a thunder cloud by simply looking upon it and bringing to bear upon mortal mind's concept of this manifestation of discord what God really has prepared for us, and she illustrated this by a wave of her hand indicating the total disappearance of the thunder cloud and its accompanying threat.[22]

Regardless of her statement that no Christian Scientist has the right to control the weather, she apparently *did* hold her students responsible for bad weather. This is illustrated by their reaction to Dickey's announcement that he had been delayed by a widespread snowstorm while traveling to Mrs. Eddy's home for the first time. Upon hearing the news, Calvin Frye stated that Mrs. Eddy should be told at once about the widespread nature of the storm. Dickey explains:

It seems that this particular snowfall had been the cause of considerable damage, and the workers in her household felt that they might be excused for their failure to control the snow if Mrs. Eddy were informed that the storm was almost country-wide and not confined to New England.[23]

One of her "watches," dated 15 January 1910, asked her workers to "make a law that there shall be no more snow this season"[24]—in New England in January!

I have offered several examples of the (seemingly) dreadful power of this unreal thing called animal magnetism. Animal magnetism casts a mystical shadow over Mrs. Eddy's otherwise utopian doctrine and gave her incredible power over her followers. It provided an explanation for anything that went wrong and a reason for changing her mind whenever it suited her. It gave her, supposedly the most spiritually minded person since Jesus, an excuse to suffer from stress, from typical symptoms of old age, and even to die—and to blame all of these problems on something other than her own spiritual failure to heal herself. It also gave her the power and justification to ultimately gain control over the entire Christian Science empire; she convinced her followers that she was the only one who could discern much of the animal magnetism attacking the Church, its leader, and its workings.

Animal magnetism and mental malpractice are not emphasized today to the degree that they were in Mrs. Eddy's time, but they still cast a subtle yet powerful shadow over Christian Scientists. Recent converts and young Christian Scientists are hardly aware of these nonexistent evils, but the evils gain importance as one becomes more deeply involved in the religion. Serious students of Christian Science usually take a two week course called "Class Instruction." A portion of the class is always dedicated to the workings of animal magnetism and instruction on combating it.[25] The students are frequently told not to tell people that they are "going through Class" until it is over, to prevent any possible mental interference during this important time of training. "Class taught" Christian Scientists who wish to become teachers must complete a "Normal Class." The class lasts not more than a week, but the subject of mental practice and malpractice consumes at least two "thorough lessons" during this time. One of the students must prepare a paper on these subjects, and then the class "thoroughly" discusses the paper. Interestingly (mystically?), the paper must then be destroyed.[26]

Christian Scientists are instructed not to pray for anyone unless specifically asked, to avoid the possibility of even unintended malpractice. A person can "clear his own thought" about someone's situation, but that is different from actually praying for the person.

Although Mrs. Eddy discussed both animal magnetism and "error" (which is just another name for animal magnetism), today's Christian Scientists use the term "error" more often than "animal magnetism." I suspect that "error" is simply easier to say and sounds less threatening than "animal magnetism." What I find interesting is the anthropomorphic powers and characteristics these non-existent illusions seem to possess: error would make us think this, or believe that. It must be guarded against and can kill a person if he believes in it—and, yet, it is unreal and only has the power that we give it. Don't try to figure this out unless you are a Christian Scientist. Circular logic only makes sense if one is safely inside the circle.

Notes

1 Mary Baker Eddy, *Science and Health*, 80:16-18; the subject is also studied twice per year in the weekly Lesson Sermon.

2 Adam H. Dickey, *Memoirs of Mary Baker Eddy* (1927; reprint, Santa Clarita, CA: The Bookmark, n.d.), 50-53.

3 I Samuel 3:9.

4 Annie M. Knott, "Reminiscences of Mary Baker Eddy," *We Knew Mary Baker Eddy*, 3rd series (Boston: The Christian Science Publishing Society, 1953), 78.

5 Adam H. Dickey, *Memoirs of Mary Baker Eddy*, 16-17; Richard A. Nenneman, *Persistent Pilgrim: The Life of Mary Baker Eddy* (Etna, NH: Nebbadoon Press, 1997), 306.

6 Mary Baker Eddy, *Science and Health*, 103:18-28.

7 Ibid., 451:26-30.

8 Robert Peel, *Mary Baker Eddy: The Years of Trial* (New York: Holt, Rinehart & Winston, 1971), 121-122.

9 Mary Baker Eddy, *The First Church of Christ Scientist and Miscellany*, 364:9-13.

10 Richard A. Nenneman, *Persistent Pilgrim: The Life of Mary Baker Eddy*, 160.

11 Willa Cather and Georgine Milmine, *The Life of Mary Baker G. Eddy & the History of Christian Science* (1909; reprint, Lincoln: University of Nebraska Press, 1993), 317.

12 Sue Harper Mims, *We Knew Mary Baker Eddy*, 2nd Series, 53, 54.

13 Robert Peel, *Mary Baker Eddy: The Years of Trial*, 94.

14 Adam H. Dickey, *Memories of Mary Baker Eddy*, 3.

15 Ibid., 12.

16 Ibid., 16-17.

17 Ibid., ix.

18 Robert Peel, *Mary Baker Eddy: The Years of Trial*, 93.

19 Ibid.

20 Martha Wilcox, "A Worker in Mrs. Eddy's Chestnut Hill Home," *We Knew Mary Baker Eddy*, 4th series (Boston: The Christian Science Publishing Society, 1972), 92.

21 Adam H. Dickey, *Memories of Mary Baker Eddy*, 19.

22 Ibid.

23 Ibid., 7.

24 Ibid., 18.

25 *Manual of The Mother Church*, ART. XXVI, SEC. 3.

26 Ibid., ART. XXX, SEC. 2.

CHAPTER EIGHT
Striving For the Impossible: Doctrine Over Person and the Demand for Purity

Experiences contradicting the group's doctrine must be ignored or reinterpreted. In matters of disagreement between the doctrine and the individual's beliefs or experience, the doctrine and group teachings are always right and the individual is always wrong.

The world is divided into good and bad, black and white. Members must continually strive to achieve unattainable purity. This impossible task inevitably produces feelings of guilt and failure.

"It begins in a nightmare, with a scream, a scream in the middle of the night that wakes me and that continues to wake me all these years later."[1] So begins Barbara Wilson's description of her mother's mental breakdown.

Barbara was ten years old when the breakdown occurred. Her mother was a devout Christian Scientist and was raising Barbara and her brother in the Church. Her father was not a Christian Scientist. He had never considered the religion to be dangerous but had just thought of Christian

Scientists as a group of nice, misguided people. Barbara's maternal grand-parents were Christian Science practitioners although her grandfather was deceased.

Barbara's mother had just gone through "Class Instruction" and awoke from a nightmare that her teacher was dead. "It's animal magnetism. I know it's animal magnetism," she cried through the worst sobbing Barbara had ever witnessed from her mother. Her father was unable to locate the teacher until the next day, but by then it was too late. Barbara's mother had suffered a complete break from reality and was unable even to recognize her frightened, bewildered children. She paced the hallway for four straight days. On the first day, Barbara tried to speak to her mother and touch her arm, but Barbara's mother brushed her aside and continued to pace. Barbara records the words her mother muttered—bits and pieces from the description of "man" in *Science and Health*.[2] In Barbara's words,

> She didn't look at me or speak to me. Instead she muttered to herself, "Man is not matter; he is not made up of brain, blood, bones and material elements." She reached the end of the hall-way and turned back again. "Man is not matter." She clasped her hands urgently together. "Man is *not* matter." She hit the opposite wall and turned. "Man is not matter, not matter, not *matter,* doesn't matter, doesn't matter, doesn't matter."[3]

A Christian Science nurse was called to take care of the pacing wom-an. She did not watch her patient closely enough to see Barbara's mother drink drain cleaner in the first of several suicide attempts. The cleaner did not kill the unfortunate woman but began to eat her face away. In a classic demonstration of the practical skills involved in Christian Science nurs-ing, the nurse called Barbara's father and asked what to do. Barbara's fa-ther called an ambulance which came and took the patient away. Barbara sums up the nightmare as follows: "One night there was a scream, and then there was four days of pacing. And then our mother was gone. We wouldn't see her again for five months."[4]

Barbara's experience is a classic example of the tragedy that can occur when a healing goes wrong. Her mother was a loving, caring, devout woman who found that she was unable to heal herself of breast cancer. She went through class instruction partly to become a practitioner, but I suspect that she was also attempting to gain a deeper understanding of Christian Science to heal her cancer. The doctors treated her emotional breakdown as a recurring psychosis "in which the individual's ability to think, respond emotionally, remember, communicate, interpret reality, and behave appropriately is sufficiently impaired so as to interfere grossly with his capacity to meet the ordinary demands of life" (Barbara's definition from a psychiatric glossary).[5]

Barbara interprets her mother's breakdown not as recurring psychosis but as a spiritual crisis. I believe that she is correct. The cancer, her secrecy about it, the timing of her class instruction, the nightmare about her teacher, and her emotional break are all too coincidental not to be related to a religious crisis. More important are the words she muttered as she paced the hall. Their progression is both instructive and haunting. "Man is not matter. . . . Man is *not* matter. . . . not *matter,* doesn't matter, doesn't matter, doesn't matter." And then she tried to kill herself.

According to Lifton, "doctrine over person" involves "the subordination of human experience to the claims of doctrine." The "demand for purity" deals with the idea that the world is divided into good and bad, black and white. Members of a group with this philosophy must continually strive for a degree of purity they can never humanly reach and which, therefore produces guilt.[6]

Barbara's mother provides a good example of both "doctrine over person" and the "demand for purity." Her religion had taught her that she was the perfect, spiritual idea of God. She sincerely believed this and was a devout, active Christian Scientist. All she had to do to obtain a healing was to better understand the "scientific truth" about herself. But understanding this "truth" meant denying the material existence of her own body and reinterpreting (spiritualizing or purifying) the sensory inputs constantly bombarding her by "mortal mind." Her relentless cancer told her that she had failed in the spiritual growth process which would have been manifested by a healing. This created incredible guilt and conflict within her, causing both the mental breakdown and her desire to kill herself.

Can Christian Science really account for the severity of the crisis Barbara's mother experienced? Consider the following excerpts from Mrs. Eddy's writings which clearly subvert the human experience and subject believers to unreasonable standards:

> Man is not matter; he is not made up of brain, blood, bones, and other material elements. The Scriptures inform us that man is made in the image and likeness of God. Matter is not that likeness. . . . Man is spiritual and perfect; and because he is spiritual and perfect, he must be so understood in Christian Science. Man is idea, the image, of Love [God]; he is not physique. . . . Man is incapable of sin, sickness, and death. . . . Mortals are the counterfeits of immortals. They are the children of the wicked one, or the one evil, which declares that man begins in dust or as a material embryo. In divine Science, God and the real man are inseparable as divine Principle and idea (*Science and Health*, 475:6-10, 11-14, 28, 476:1-5).

> Error, urged to its final limits, is self-destroyed. . . . Sin, sickness, and death must disappear to give place to the facts which belong to immortal man. Learn this, O mortal, and earnestly seek the spiritual status of man, which is outside of all material selfhood. . . . To the five corporeal senses, man appears to be matter and mind united; but Christian Science reveals man as the idea of God, and declares the corporeal senses to be mortal and erring illusions. Divine Science shows it to be impossible that a material body, though interwoven with matter's highest stratum, misnamed mind, should be man,—the genuine and perfect man, the immortal idea of being, indestructible and eternal. Were it otherwise, man would be annihilated (*Science and Health*, 476:6, 18-22, 477:9-18).

The sick are not healed merely by declaring there is no sickness, but by knowing that there is none (*Science and Health*, 447:27-29).

Usually to admit that you are sick, renders your case less curable. . . . to prove scientifically the error or unreality of disease, you must mentally unsee the disease; then you will not feel it, and it is destroyed (*Science and Health*, 461:21-22,28-30).

Science speaks when the senses are silent. . . . Christian Science and the senses are at war. . . . He who turns to the body for evidence, bases his conclusions on mortality, on imperfection. . . . (*Miscellaneous Writings*, 100:19, 101:8, 19-20).

If God is all, and God is good, it follows that all must be good; and no other power, law, or intelligence can exist. On this proof rest premise and conclusion in Science, and the facts that disprove the evidence of the senses (*Miscellaneous Writings*, 101:26-30).

Human pity often brings pain. . . . Science supports harmony, denies suffering, and destroys it with the divinity of Truth. . . . Nothing appears to the physical senses but their own subjective state of thought. The senses join issue with error, and pity what has no right either to be pitied or to exist, and what does not exist in Science. Destroy the thought of sin, sickness, death, and you destroy their existence (*Miscellaneous Writings*, 102:21-24, 105:24-29).

It is no more Christianly scientific to see disease than it is to experience it. If you would destroy the sense of disease, you should not build it up by wishing to see the forms it assumes or by employing a single material application for its relief (*Science and Health*, 421:25-30).

The above sampling of Mrs. Eddy's statements illustrates the incredible disparity between what a Christian Scientist sees and feels, and how he or she must revise sensory inputs into a new reality which meshes with that of Christian Science. To do any less—to acknowledge the physical problem or, worse, to have it treated medically—is to deny spiritual truth, to undermine the basis of one's faith, and to make future healings more difficult.

Barbara's mother was not inherently insane; she just could not reconcile her strong belief in Christian Science with her inability to heal her cancer. She understood the futility and spiritual danger of believing in a material existence and in the reality of her physical body. Yet, she had failed in her Christian Science "demonstration" over them. She was crushed by what she undoubtedly perceived to be her spiritual failure and immaturity. These realizations crashed upon her as she paced the hall and muttered, "man is not matter.... Man is *not* matter ... not *matter,* doesn't matter, doesn't matter...." Notice the desperation, guilt, and despair in these statements; her attempt to reach the Christian Science standard of purity in the first statements, followed by her sense of guilt and worthlessness in the latter phrases. And then she drank drain cleaner.

Barbara's mother is not alone. She exemplifies thousands of sincere Christian Scientists who firmly believe in their religion, practice it for years, and finally encounter a problem they "cannot handle." Most do not react as severely as Barbara's mother. Some lose their faith and leave Christian Science, often carrying a tremendous sense of loss, failure, and betrayal along with them. Others simply ignore the problem and suffer whatever consequences ensue. Many remain within the church but finally go to the doctor, although it is taught that seeking medical help will make subsequent healings more difficult. Those who do seek medical care find ways to emotionally justify their actions, and they usually keep them a secret to protect the reputation of Christian Science and avoid having to admit the issue to other believers.

An Impossible Dilemma

Perhaps the most unfortunate group of believers includes the most devout—those who follow Mrs. Eddy's teachings of "radical reliance" on Christian Science. Before we discuss these people I should acknowledge that neither Mrs. Eddy nor her followers recommend carrying an unsuccessful healing to the point of death. I frequently heard and repeated the following comment during my years in Christian Science: "Of course, a Christian Scientist shouldn't let himself or his child die. If you can't handle a problem, go to a doctor!" (Note the implied failure in this accommodating statement.) Mrs. Eddy consented to medical care for problems like contagious disease, broken bones, and surgery, stating that these concessions can be made until the world is more "ready" to accept Christian Science even though Christian Science is perfectly capable of healing the problems.[7] She also allowed pain killers to be used if the pain was so great that it prevented the patient from thinking metaphysically[8] (she herself resorted to morphine upon occasion).

Mrs. Eddy recommended that Christian Scientists "emerge gently from matter into Spirit,[9]" implying that one should not tackle seemingly difficult medical problems until one has gained enough spiritual understanding to handle them. But her advice to emerge gently is eclipsed by other statements that pressure Christian Scientists into avoiding medical help and which even cause many to fear the medical profession. Mrs. Eddy made far more statements against medicine, health-related hygiene, and any kind of reliance on physical help than she made in favor of them. She also taught that directly confronting the evidence of the physical senses was the best way to overcome it. She placed her students in an almost impossible dilemma—do not tackle what you are not ready for, but you will never learn Christian Science unless you follow its teachings exactly, taking a firm stand against medicine and materiality. Consider a few more of Mrs. Eddy's comments regarding disease and medicine:

It is plain that God does not employ drugs or hygiene, nor provide them for human use; else Jesus would have recommended and employed them in his healing (*Science and Health*, 143:5-8).

Drugs and hygiene oppose the supremacy of the divine Mind. Drugs and inert matter are unconscious, mindless. Certain results, supposed to proceed from drugs, are really caused by the faith in them which the false human consciousness is educated to feel (*Science and Health*, 484:15-20).

A physical diagnosis of disease—since mortal mind must be the cause of disease— tends to induce disease (*Science and Health*, 370:20-22).

A patient thoroughly booked in medical theories is more difficult to heal through Mind than one who is not (*Science and Health*, 382:19-21).

One who understands Christian Science can heal the sick . . . and this practical proof is the only feasible evidence that one does understand this Science (*Science and Health*, 345:17-20).

Declare that you are not hurt and understand the reason why. . . . (*Science and Health*, 397:17-18).

. . . the Christian Scientist takes the best care of his body when he leaves it most out of his thought, and, like the Apostle Paul, is "willing rather to be absent from the body, and to be present with the Lord" (*Science and Health*, 383:7-11).

Add the following pressures and inducements to Mrs. Eddy's statements:

- Christian Science heavily emphasizes healings. Testimonies of healing are presented in all Christian Science periodicals, at Wednesday night testimony meetings, and at major church-sponsored meetings. (Keep in mind that most of these healed conditions are never medically diagnosed, that symptoms are usually not discussed during the testimonies, and that Christian Scientists generally know very little about anatomy or medicine. While some healings sound truly miraculous and a few involve medically documented cases, one has to wonder whether most of them would have occurred naturally without Christian Science treatment. Christian Scientists usually assume that the healings are valid, despite their lack of medical proof.)

- Christian Scientists are thrilled by testimonies in which people are healed from what seem to be "death-bed" situations. Healing is always just around the corner if the Christian Scientist will study Mrs. Eddy's writings a little harder—understand the Truth a little more clearly—stick with it a little longer . . .

- Christian Scientists having trouble with a healing are encouraged to employ the aid of a practitioner. A practitioner is a Christian Scientist whose profession is to help other people obtain healings. His or her job is to convince the patient—to "help the patient understand"—that he or she is not really sick or hurt but is the perfect, spiritual idea of God. Patients who decide to seek medical help are immediately abandoned by their practitioners since Christian Science and medicine cannot be employed simultaneously. Choosing to see a doctor is difficult once one is under the care of a practitioner.

- Believers are taught not to worry if their symptoms seem to worsen during Christian Science treatment or while reading *Science and Health*. They are taught that the emotional or physical discomfort is often caused by what Mrs. Eddy calls "chemicalization." Chemicalization is "the process which mortal mind and body undergo in the change of belief from a material to a spiritual basis." Mrs. Eddy compares it to an alkali destroying an acid and even suggests that the aggravation of certain symptoms is a sign of spiritual progress.[10] Chemicalization is an extremely dangerous concept since it can suggest that a patient is improving when the disease is actually getting worse. This often delays a person's decision to seek medical care until it is too late. If the person does finally go to the doctor at the last minute and then dies, the death is blamed on the doctor and the patient rather than on Christian Science.

- Christian Science teaches parents that their thinking directly affects their children's health. One of Mrs. Eddy's students once asked her why his child had a cold. Her emphatic response was that the man had caught cold for his son.[11] Parents can face difficult choices when a child becomes seriously ill. They want to set a good spiritual example by healing the problem through Christian Science, but sometimes the illness becomes quite frightening or prolonged. Then the parents are faced with a dilemma; taking their child to the doctor might solve the problem but will hinder their spiritual growth and might spiritually confuse their child. Sticking with Christian Science may end in tragedy. There is no easy way out.

Because of the standards and inducements described above, devout believers frequently stick with Christian Science beyond reason and end up inadvertently neglecting and abusing themselves or their children. A few case histories will illustrate the fact. Most of these stories describe the experiences of normal, loving people who were simply trying to practice their faith. Unless linked to a reference, the names have been changed since I know many of these people or have heard of them from friends. Lest the reader think I am trying to sensationalize, let me comment that I have excluded several tragic and revealing case histories to protect the privacy or emotions of the people involved. Some things are just too private to put in a book, even under an assumed name. Consider the following cases:

- Judy was a teenager when she contracted what she now suspects was pneumonia. She missed a month of school, experienced constant pain and frequent fainting spells, and lost 35 pounds as her parents and practitioner prayed to know that she was well.

She finally recovered after several weeks and was declared to be healed. In her words, "it didn't seem like [a healing] to me."

- Another teenage girl in Judy's Sunday school choked to death on her own tonsils.

- Jim had athletes' foot. The condition lasted for weeks or months and itched so badly that he would lie in bed and scratch his feet until they bled. Jim was never given any relief for the itching.

- Lisa was dying of an incurable disease, but her family refused to acknowledge the problem. The child was never given the emotional support that any human being would need under the circumstances. A few days before her death she was still being propped up at the dinner table, semi-conscious, so the family could eat together.

- Chuck was a middle-aged man in my church. He bore a huge, horrible growth on the side of his head for either months or years (I cannot remember the exact length of time). I used to be fascinated that he always wore one small bandage in the middle of the mass. It was dwarfed by the horrible growth but must have been there to catch some perpetual oozing. At some point he disappeared from church and I was told that he had died.

- Tim had a childhood friend, John, who received a large gash on his head as the boys played together. Tim's mother bandaged John's head and then Tim escorted him home. John's mother took one look at him, ripped the bandage from his head, and told him to go play because he was not hurt. He developed a large scar where the gash had been.

- Marie had a schoolmate who received a head wound which kept swelling to a greater and greater size. He would have died had a school official not stepped in and gotten medical help for the boy.

- Sarah and her younger brother Brian grew up in a devout Christian Science family. Sarah resented that her parents gave Brian special attention and pampering. Not until the children grew up was the truth revealed that Brian had diabetes. He had been under medical care for years, but even his siblings did not know it.

- In her article, "Suffering Children and the Christian Science Church," Caroline Fraser describes trying to avoid car sickness as a very young child. She would repeatedly declare, "I am God's perfect child." Christian Scientists typically cling to this "truth" as they try to heal themselves (it took me years to get the phrase out of my head). Caroline would inevitably throw up anyway and her angry father would yell, "You're going to have to learn not to do that!" Caroline continues, "my father was a particularly zealous Christian Scientist, but young Christian Science children, who have little choice but to believe what their parents are telling them, are taught that illness originates in errors in their parents' and eventually their own thinking. So for them, sickness becomes an experience of self-doubt, anxiety, and shame."[12]

- I attended Principia College and took the very popular course "The History of the Christian Science Movement." The teacher was a wonderful middle-aged woman whose spiritual strength was clear and inspiring as she taught the course about our religion and its leader. My teacher had a large goiter on her neck which suggested a thyroid problem. To my knowledge she never healed the problem and we never mentioned it. She died just before my fifth-year class reunion. Of course, I knew not to ask why. Interestingly, the only other goiter I have seen was also on a Christian Scientist. A friend also mentioned that she had seen a woman with a goiter and had remarked to her husband that the woman must be a Christian Scientist. Sure enough, they later saw the woman in a Christian Science reading room. My friend commented to her husband that no one but a Christian Scientist would put up with such a thing!

- I took a gym class at my Christian Science college. The temperature was set too high on the squash courts, and the heat was making me sick. I explained my problem to my instructor and asked that he lower the thermostat by a couple of degrees.

He refused with the comment, "Just overcome it!" I wondered why this had to become a spiritual issue when it would have been easier to turn down the thermostat.

- Mary attended my college and lived in an on-campus dormitory. The dorm rooms had no locks in order to encourage a family feeling on campus. The unlocked doors did not usually pose a problem but, for a time, there was a theft problem. Mary lost several items and complained to her "house mom." Her house mom told her that things were being stolen from her because of problems in her thinking.

- Mike lost his first wife to untreated cancer. He remarried and his second wife died of a skin cancer which ate a large, rotten hole in her chest.

- H.R. Haldeman, a former cabinet member for President Nixon, developed a stomach ailment which lasted for weeks. His son, Peter, reports that Haldeman was so sick that he could only eat ice chips. He died under Christian Science care without ever seeking medical help. Fearing that the press might become interested in the event, his family negotiated with the coroner to list a cause of death that would not be damaging to Christian Science.[13]

- During graduate school, I belonged to an organization for Christian Science students. Amy was a very devout member of our group. She was suffering from an ailment which seemed to somehow involve blood. The problem went on for some time and Amy occasionally made vague comments like "my parents said that if I don't get this thing healed I'm going to have to have an operation." It was clear to me that she desperately needed for someone to ask her about the ailment and to lend emotional support. I longed to ask what was wrong, but refrained because of the pressure not to "make a reality" of something by talking about it. As far as I know, Amy suffered alone within the Christian Science group at a time when she really needed our help.

- Janet's non-Christian Science father was badly injured in an accident when she was a young adult. He was treated in a hospital

and, despite her Christian Science mother's disapproval, she
visited him a week after the accident. In Janet's words, "his
head was twice the size, black and blue, tubes, casts, all kinds of
machines around him in Intensive Care. The only way I knew
it was my dad was because I recognized his fingertips. Yet, as a
good C[hristian] S[cientist], I had to deny all I saw and 'know'
that my dad was perfect and 'know' nothing was wrong with
him. And I needed to keep working in my mind to overcome this
'seeming' horror and maintain the correct thoughts so dad would
be healed." Imagine Janet's mental gymnastics as she repeatedly
translated her sensory inputs into Christian Science thinking.

- Maria was a fairly new Christian Scientist whose dear friend,
John, fell and sustained serious injuries (he suffered two broken
legs, a broken shoulder and wrist, and cracked ribs. One leg
required pins, screws, bolts, and stitches from his foot to above
his knee. He also required reconstructive surgery on his ankle.)
John was not a Christian Scientist. When Maria told her Christian
Science mentor, Mike, about the accident and asked what she
should do, Mike told her, "the radical spiritual truth that applies
is that [John] never fell!" Maria now laments, "this is a dreadful
admission. When [Mike] told me about seeing [John] as an
'unfallen man'—I actually did that. I still remember . . . it is so real.
. . . I went to see [John] with bones in his leg so shattered. Some
were beyond repair, his ankle needing to be rebuilt, a broken
wrist, bruises and bumps, and I 'saw' him as a perfect and whole
man just as God had created him. I could look past the hurting
man in dreadful pain (who has a very high tolerance for pain)
and say to him, 'you are okay now!' Oh, I cringe as I write this. . .
." Now that she is out of Christian Science, Maria is horrified by
how insensitive her belief system made her toward John's need
for genuine, gut-level validation and encouragement during his
time of need. By the way, I happened upon a testimony in the July
1898 Christian Science Journal which describes the healing of a
little girl after a fall. The title of the article is, "She Never Fell."

- When I was sixteen-years-old, I badly sprained my ankle during a ski trip sponsored by our local Adventure Unlimited group (a group for Christian Science youth). My binding failed to release during a fall and I ended up face down in the snow with my ski stuck in the snow, pointing in the wrong direction. The fall left me screaming in pain. I was carried into the lodge and we spent several agonizing minutes removing my ski boot. Before long I was approached by a well-known practitioner who was helping to chaperone our group. He sat beside me and we began to "know the truth" about the situation. We sat quietly for a few minutes and then he asked, "Shall we go for a walk?" I had been told that he was a successful healer and I was eager for spiritual growth, so I agreed to go with him. We spent a great deal of effort putting on my own boot because of my intense discomfort. Then we took a long walk up and down the mountain road. It was a slow and agonizing walk, but we defied the physical evidence of the situation and "knew" that I was a perfect child of God who could not really be hurt. I felt a certain excitement because I was going through a healing with a renowned practitioner. What a chance to learn and to grow spiritually!

That night another chaperone sat with me as I lay in bed in great pain. She described a spectacular healing she had experienced after a car accident. Her healing encouraged me to continue declaring the unreality of my own injury. We never wrapped my ankle or even put ice on it despite its swelling and great discoloration. My parents were never notified of the accident. We returned home the next day and then I walked all over my two-story high school without ever wrapping the ankle or using crutches. I was quite embarrassed about my obvious limp since my non-Science friends had challenged me with the classic "what if you break your leg?" question the day before the trip. I had confidently explained the process of Christian Science treatment to them . . . and now, here I was, doing my best to hide my obvious limp and to heal the ankle.

The swelling subsided after several days and so my parents, practitioner, and I concluded that the healing was well underway.

Later that summer I took a two week backpacking trip through the Rocky Mountains—proof that my ankle was strong and healed. There is only one problem with this "healing." My ankle hurt for at least a month after the accident and has never been quite the same.

The case histories above are representative of many tragedies and misfortunes I could describe. They illustrate the danger, needless suffering, and poor judgment often involved in Christian Science healing. These abuses usually occur out of ignorance, in the name of love, and with a sincere desire to grow spiritually. They are usually not the product of fanaticism but are a natural result of Christian Science doctrine as illustrated earlier by some of Mrs. Eddy's statements. While in Christian Science I heard stories about failed healings and passed them off as anomalies within the great sea of Christian Science successes. Now that I am out I realize that I heard, saw, and experienced too many of these failed healings to honestly classify them as anomalies.

Return to Lifton

Consider Lifton's criteria for thought reform and what he calls "doctrine over person" and the "demand for purity." By now it should be clear that Christian Science is infested by these criteria. First, the doctrine is absolute and leaves little room for original thought. As Mrs. Eddy said, "in reality there is, and can be, but one school of the Science of Mind-healing. . . . A slight divergence is fatal [to success] in Science."[14] Second, Christian Science claims that the material world is unreal and that a person's physical senses are defective. These claims destroy the usual reference points from which a person shapes his or her personality and world view. They force the believer to reinterpret reality and to deny emotions that do not mesh with Christian Science doctrine. Believers must submit their basic humanity to the requirements of Christian Science. This explains why believers can put themselves and their loved ones through all manner of suffering in the name of healing. The human part of them which should scream, "Stop! This suffering is crazy!" is suppressed. They are not allowed to believe that the suffering exists lest they *give* it some kind of reality.

There is no middle road; matter either exists or it does not exist. Those who are completely committed to the Christian Science way of thinking lead contented lives whether they remain healthy or suffer terribly. Those who are not fully convinced that matter is unreal live on a kind of fence, alternating between a sense of victory when things go well and terrible inadequacy when they face a problem they cannot overcome. The walk along this fence can be frustrating and even maddening. This maddening fence is typical in groups which control the hearts and minds of their members. Those who fully believe the groups' teachings are happy even in the midst of suffering. Those who have doubts range from mildly discontented to miserable.

Christian Science is different from the more obvious mind-control groups. It does not need to break its members' wills with overwork, poor food, and other excessive controls involving their everyday activities. Christian Science simply offers some irresistible carrots—absolute truth, healings, a foolproof way to overcome life's problems, guaranteed salvation—and people buy into the system. Those who believe they are healed through Christian Science are usually hooked. They often cling to one experience even if they never have another healing—one can attend Wednesday night testimony meetings and hear people tell of healings that happened in the distant past. Christian Science captures the mind and produces smiling, optimistic people who hide their problems and usually do not admit their spiritual failures. That is why it is so difficult for outsiders to identify this religion's controlling and damaging nature. Most of it is subtle, secret, and hidden behind smiles and open optimism.

The writings of early Christian Scientists are sprinkled with anecdotes and comments revealing how their true feelings are subjugated to Christian Science doctrine. This submission is not surprising since it is commanded throughout Mrs. Eddy's writings and teachings. I find one of her comments to Adam Dickey especially interesting since it reminds me of my practitioner's instructions after my skiing accident. Mrs. Eddy made the statement after "demonstrating" over the belief in arthritis before a carriage ride:

> whenever anything happens to you of an unfortunate nature, do not admit anything on the wrong side, but instantly declare that the experience does you good. Even if you should fall down and break your leg, get up and say, I am better for this experience. This is the Truth as God would declare it.[15]

(And so the practitioner had me get up and walk on the badly sprained ankle to prove that my "true," spiritual being could not be injured . . .)

Christian Science tends to separate a person's mind and body in a form of mild, but almost constant, dissociation. This is a natural goal for any religion that teaches its members to strive for a wholly spiritual state of consciousness. Most Christian Scientists would be offended if they were accused of applauding dissociation, but the goal is beautifully illustrated by an incident which occurred when a friend took class instruction from Herbert Rieke in 1966. The teacher was not present at the time, but several class members spent part of an evening singing around a piano. One of the songs they sang gives a clear picture of the mental attitude fostered within the class. The song is a take-off on the classic "My Bonnie Lies Over the Ocean." The Christian Scientists sang it like this:

> My *body* lies over the ocean
> My *body* lies over the sea
> My *body* lies over the ocean
> *Don't* bring back my *body* to me
>
> *Don't bring, don't bring*
> *Don't bring back my body to me, to me*
> *Don't bring, don't bring*
> *Don't bring back my body to me*

Mrs. Eddy revealed her own dissociation when she pointed out the place where "Mary" was born but said that she had never been born.

The Plight of Children

The most unfortunate victims of Christian Science doctrine are often the children of devout, well-meaning parents. They must live with a belief system telling them that their bodies and the world around them are an illusion. This abstract concept is impossible for a child to understand. It can produce both guilt and confusion in a child who feels physical sensation but must deny it and who must learn to reinterpret events which seem very real. Barbara Wilson describes the feeling:

> To have a body—I knew this deeply, without thinking—was to touch and taste and smell your way through a world that was endlessly rich and varied. But in my metaphysical childhood, to have a body was also to have a kind of enemy scout between your mind and Divine Mind, a secret agent whose dispatches from the physical world had to be ignored at all costs. You couldn't have thought this up on your own, not as a child; you couldn't have learned to treat your senses as treacherous. It was a system thought up by an adult. . . .

Barbara then brings up an interesting irony:

> But I did know, without understanding, that you had to have a thing in front of you to realize that it was not really a thing. You had to see a bird to know it wasn't there....[16]

Janet describes her confusion as a young child in Sunday school:

> I was sitting in a Sunday School class at a table by the window. I remember my teacher saying that the table we were sitting

at was unreal and only an illusion. So was the tree outside the window. I remember thinking to myself that they look pretty real to me, but that I better not tell anyone what I was thinking or they would think I was spiritually inferior.

Barbara and Janet have illustrated a serious issue undermining the self-confidence and emotional health of many Christian Science children. The issue is obvious: the need for validation. The gut-level desire for one's emotions, sensory inputs, and needs to be taken seriously. A person needs only to watch a group of young children at play to understand the importance of validation. When children hurt themselves they run to their parents to have the pain acknowledged. Often a child simply shows the bump to her mother, receives a kiss and some loving words regarding the injury, and then happily returns to her game. The love and kiss cannot heal the bump, but they are so important to the child that she will often cry and act hurt until she receives them. This desire to have pain acknowledged is almost universal among children and adults. Christian Scientists deprive themselves and their children of this basic human need because they cannot admit that pain is real. I have discussed the validation issue with a number of people who grew up in Christian Science and have seen many of them reduced to tears. They obviously identify with the problem. David's comments illustrate what can happen when a child's needs and emotions are not properly validated:

> I think of my childhood as if I were a little boy—five or six years old, lost on top of a mountain in the fog, alone, cold, frightened and confused—but mostly alone. This is the metaphor that I developed to describe my Christian Science-bound childhood. . . . I was subtly and profoundly abused.

The "lonely child" still cries inside many adults who grew up in Christian Science.

Despite the confusion, guilt, and non-existent validation, Christian Science children often lead contented lives because their religion teaches them to be optimistic and to see themselves as spiritually perfect, religiously superior, and able to overcome life's seeming trials. In a sense they are taught to simultaneously live in two separate realities; they play, eat, and experience the ups and downs of life in the physical illusion around them while metaphysically filtering out the unpleasant aspects of their lives by "knowing the truth" about their true spiritual existence. In other words, they learn to live with selective denial and to internalize only the good in life. That works to a point, but Christian Scientists often grow up with insecurities and emotional scars that could have been avoided by acknowledging and dealing with life's problems as they arose, instead of brushing them under the metaphysical rug. Some people struggle with the scars for a lifetime without understanding their origin. Others never recognize the damage, but it leaks out in the form of insecurity, a general lack of empathy, and emotional difficulties such as misplaced anger.

In my case, I led a contented childhood and then experienced tremendous emotional fallout after I left the religion and began to examine my past without any metaphysical filters. I had to sort through a lifetime of confused and angry emotions, dealing with events ranging from minor inconveniences to major traumas. I was truly surprised at the intensity of my anger over certain events. I am convinced that they would have been less traumatic had I been allowed to deal with them as they happened, instead of many years later and with a mass of other memories.

I was fortunate. I did not lose any family members to Christian Science and did not face any devastating illnesses myself. Those children who do experience illness can suffer mercilessly at the well-meaning hands of those who love them the most. These children are frequently the offspring of practitioners—the paid healers and spiritual guides among the Christian Science community. Practitioners are used to denying and ignoring all manner of physical problems and so usually do the same with their children. Furthermore, they have more to lose than the average Christian Scientist who finally goes to the doctor; they are bound by their professions.

Beth's mother was a practitioner. One day Beth put her hand through a glass door while chasing a friend who had taken her toy. She cut her hand to the bone, leaving the fourth finger hanging backwards. Beth's mother was angry because the little girl's "evil thoughts had caused the accident." She told Beth to raise the bleeding hand above her head and commanded her *not* to faint. After driving an hour toward home, Beth's mother stopped at a pay-phone and spent another thirty minutes consulting with a practitioner friend. As the two women talked the child sat in the car alone, in pain, frightened, and bleeding. Finally her mother decided to have the hand bandaged by a doctor. She did not allow stitches and pain killers, but permitted the hand to be bandaged in a cupped position to stop the bleeding. Then she was angry when Beth needed help getting dressed because of the bandage. But Beth was used to being blamed for having normal, everyday problems. For example, she was frequently sent to school with flu-like symptoms and was chastised by her teacher for spreading germs. Her mother would then be angry because Beth could not heal herself. For Beth, it was normal to be stuck in impossible circumstances.

Some practitioners finally realize that their Christian Science treatments can lead to inadvertent child abuse. Suzanne is one of those individuals who finally saw what she was doing and had the courage to stand up to the "system." Both her childhood and adult experiences illustrate the neglect and damage that Christian Scientists can impose upon each other in the name of healing, so it is worth recounting a portion of her story. A more complete account was published an article entitled, "Suffer the Little Children."[17] In this article, Suzanne describes her Christian Science childhood and recalls how her parents and practitioner treated her when she was sick.

> Whenever I complained that I didn't feel well, Mom would tell me, "Now go lie down. You're all right." She'd call our practitioner, who'd tell me my sickness wasn't real. And Dad would quote from the Bible, "Physician, heal thyself," meaning that since God was the only physician, and I was the child of God, I could heal myself from within.

Suzanne also recalls how her grandfather was kept on a cot in the basement when he became ill with open sores. One of the sores had eaten a hole through his cheek and she could see "teeth, tongue, jaw, and drool coming out of it."[18] Suzanne's grandpa died but the eight-year-old girl was not allowed to grieve.

Suzanne was seriously injured in a gymnastics accident and, for two weeks, was paralyzed from the neck down. It took months to recover from the accident and she still suffers some aftereffects, but it never occurred to her or anyone else in her family to seek medical care for this serious accident.

Suzanne's mother died a slow and terrible death from ovarian cancer. She resisted going to a doctor despite the pain and her badly swollen stomach; her practitioner kept reassuring her that nothing was wrong. She finally shocked her family by going to a doctor because the pain was unbearable. The only medical care she received was to have the tumor drained, but a practitioner told her that getting a diagnosis would prevent her from healing. Suzanne's mother was then denied entrance into a Christian Science nursing home because she had been to a doctor within the past year. She died an agonizing death without the support of her church.

Suzanne's story continues as she describes experiences involving her own children. They attended a Christian Science school, and one day her four-year-old son was sent home with a note that she needed to pray for him. Suzanne called the school and was told that he had whined all day. She later undressed the child and discovered a broken collar bone. Apparently, no one at school had investigated the reason for the little boy's unhappiness. Perhaps Suzanne's worst memory involves a week in 1986 when her young daughter's appendix burst. She diligently prayed and cared for Marilyn for three days before the child slipped into a coma. Even as Marilyn was vomiting "black gunk," her practitioner kept telling Suzanne that there was nothing wrong. Suzanne finally rushed her child to a hospital, after which the practitioner told her that it would have been better to let Marilyn die than to seek medical help. Some of her Christian

Science friends found her and tried to convince her not to allow the doctors to operate on the girl, who by this time also had peritonitis. Suzanne recalls, "two came rushing into the waiting room and begged me to take Marilyn home. 'She's on the operating table,' I said. One woman told me, 'they can sew her up. You still have the legal right to take her out.' "

Suzanne remained a practitioner for a time, hoping to convince people that there is a time to seek medical care for one's children. She resigned when she realized that she could not change the system and that children would continue to die. Finally, in 1992, another death convinced her that it was time to speak out. She told her story to a local newspaper and was amazed by the response.

> I wasn't prepared for the hundreds of letters and phone calls from Christian Science parents after the article was published. Most were anonymous, as their writers feared reprisals from the church. All told heartbreaking stories of untreated sicknesses and death. And many confessed to secretly going to doctors to get help for their children. I no longer felt alone.

Suzanne's church excommunicated her in 1993.

I have listened to the stories of many Christian Science survivors, as some of them prefer to be called, and have been horrified by what these children went through in the name of "healing." Many were punished for being sick and for not responding to the truth being preached to them; others were placed in rooms by themselves with a copy of *Science and Health*. They were isolated at a time when they most needed to be cuddled and nurtured. In other cases, children had to watch siblings die slow, painful deaths and were not allowed to acknowledge the problem, much less to grieve. Most of these were the children of loving, well-meaning parents trapped in the belief that Christian Science was the best, most reliable treatment for their children—if only they understood it well enough.

Many articles have been published describing the plight of children in Christian Science and other sects that shun medical care. Several resources are listed in the endnotes.[19]

I was lucky. I had very supportive parents and could tell them about my problems. But, no matter how "down to earth" our discussions were, they usually ended with my father assuring me, with great love, "but we know that this is no part of you." With his declaration, any gut-level validation I had felt would vanish. I guess I wasn't so lucky after all. It took years to figure out why a little part of me felt so horribly alone.

And in Mrs. Eddy's Day?

Christian Science doctrine has changed very little since Mrs. Eddy's time because her writings are considered infallible and cannot be altered. Sincere Christian Scientists were losing their humanity in the doctrine and striving for perfection in Mrs. Eddy's day at least as much as they are today. A highlighted quote in the April 1898 Christian Science Journal provides some insight into how believers dealt with their problems. According to the Poughkeepsie Daily Eagle:

> There is one very good thing about the Christian Scientists. When they feel sick they don't talk about it. Sickness is the great staple of conversation among many other people, and it would be a great gain if it could be superseded by something more elevating.[20]

While it is true that people often talk too much about their problems, emphasizing that it is good to remain silent reinforces a Christian Science practice that often produces deep emotional scars. In printing the statement without further comment, the *Christian Science Journal* editors ignore the very human fact that sometimes illness *needs* to be talked about.

It is interesting to look at some examples of how Mrs. Eddy and her most trusted students dealt with their problems.

- Mrs. Eddy mourned essentially alone after her third husband was "mentally murdered."[21]
- One of Mrs. Eddy's students went hungry during a time when few people asked for her services as a practitioner. She felt that she

had to work through the problem alone ("it was my problem to solve"), so she suffered in silence until the lean time passed.[22]

- One of Mrs. Eddy's students lost two children under Christian Science treatment "with hardly a murmur."[23]

- Calvin Frye, who served Mrs. Eddy for nearly twenty-eight years, lost interest in family ties and showed little concern upon losing his father and sister. When his father died four years after he began serving Mrs. Eddy, he made a brief appearance at the funeral. Frye did not acknowledge his sister's demise four years later. He ignored her death, the funeral, and his family's request for a little money to help with the burial. As Cather puts it, "for him family ties no longer existed, and death had become merely a belief."[24]

The Perils of Personality

Personality—individuality, choice, good thoughts, and bad thoughts. The things that make us human—these are dangerous to Christian Science.

Christian Science teaches that we are all the spiritual reflections of God—Mind. As such, "thought passes from God to man, but neither sensation nor report goes from material body to Mind."[25] Notice that in this statement man is allowed to keep the name "man" when God's thoughts are passing to him, but he becomes a mere "material body" when he tries to think for himself. He is a spiritual reflection of God in the first part of the sentence but sinks to a material counterfeit in the second part of the sentence. He is not allowed to be an individually-created being with a God-given mind. If he is not a spiritual being reflecting the "one Mind" that everyone else reflects, he is simply a material illusion.

Christian Science tolerates personality only when it is part of the "one Mind." This way, everything is spiritual and good and harmonious. Mrs. Eddy believed that all evil (error, mesmerism, or animal magnetism) originates from a belief that there are minds apart from God. She believed that these so-called minds dreamed up the illusions of sin, sickness, and death. She never really explained the origin of these illusions since God is all and wholly good. But error—mesmerism and animal magnetism—can be murderous. The logic is mind-boggling; evil is unreal but can kill you if you believe that it has power. Even if you do not believe that it has power (as Mrs. Eddy did not), you still have to mentally guard against it so it will not hurt you.

Christian Scientists generally consider themselves to be free-thinking individuals. They do not realize how their personalities are stifled as they reinterpret negative events to prevent error from taking hold in their thoughts. They cannot truly feel their emotions because their senses cannot be trusted. When sick or sad they must deny their true emotions in order to clear the way for spiritual healing. They cannot pray for one another unless asked because their thoughts can harm another person even when they mean well. Everything must be spiritualized.

In her "Message for 1901," Mrs. Eddy posed the question, "do Christian Scientists believe in personality?" She answered:

> [26]They do, but their personality is defined spiritually, not mate-rially—by Mind, not by matter. We do not blot out the material race of Adam, but leave all sin to God's fiat—self-extinction, and to the final manifestation of the real spiritual man and universe. We believe, according to the Scriptures, that God is infinite Spirit or Person, and man is His image and likeness: therefore man reflects Spirit, not matter.

In other words, "no, Christian Scientists do not believe in personal-ity as the rest of the world defines it. We have made our own definition so that we will think that we believe in personality." Perhaps the most revealing evidence for the subversion of personality was Mrs. Eddy's at-titude about her own personality. She constantly struggled with the idea that malicious animal magnetism was out to destroy her. Since animal magnetism involves the thoughts of others, she did not allow people to concentrate on her personality. Martha Wilcox, a member of Mrs. Eddy's household, wrote:

never for one minute were we allowed to let our thought rest upon her personality. We understood that that would be a hindrance to her. It was her instructions to us that were paramount—so much so that we could be in the house for weeks and not think of her personality.[27]

Mrs. Wilcox remembers that her first conversation with Mrs. Eddy (after joining the household) involved the subject of mental malpractice. What is so interesting about this lesson is Mrs. Wilcox's reaction to it. She states, "this lesson on mental malpractice was quite apropos for one entering a household comprised of never less than 17 up to 25 so-called personalities."[28] First, notice that she refers to the other people as "so-called" personalities instead of as people. Second, keep in mind that these so-called personalities represented Mrs. Eddy's best students, hand-picked from all over the country. If *these* people represented a threat, what must the rest of the world be like? Certainly, personality was something to be avoided.

Emma Newman quotes Mrs. Eddy's description of her first visit to The Mother Church on 26 May 1895. Mrs. Eddy said, "I discerned every mentality there, but saw no personality." Mrs. Newman noted, "this gave us an enlarged and wonderful sense of what spiritual discernment was, in contrast with the earth-weighted sense of personality."[29]

Perfection at Its Best

Mrs. Eddy's demand for purity included an interesting aspect. She was an extreme perfectionist and required the same of her students. According to Martha Wilcox, "Mrs. Eddy believed that if one's thought was not orderly and exact in the things that make up present consciousness, that same thought would not be exact enough to give a treatment or use an exact science." Mrs. Wilcox suggests that Mrs. Eddy's perfectionism showed, to an unusual degree, "the exactness and divine order of God—her Mind. . . ." With true admiration, Mrs. Wilcox admits that

Mrs. Eddy's degree of perfectionism was far beyond her "so-called" human comprehension.[30]

Mrs. Eddy demanded that items in her home remain exactly as she originally had them placed. As discussed in chapter four, she was so sensitive to this issue that her workers finally set a tack under each item so it could be maintained in its precisely designated location.[31] Mrs. Eddy also required that meals be served exactly on time and perfectly cooked. Even her pin cushion was in perfect order, and no one would have considered moving one of the pins.[32]

Mrs. Eddy also expected her workers to know where items were located in the house when she, herself, had not seen them for years and her workers had *never* seen them. Mrs. Wilcox justifies this impossible standard with the statement,

> And, why not, when consciousness includes all. [Mrs. Eddy] taught me that there was only one consciousness, and that this consciousness was my consciousness and included all ideas as present and at hand and she expected me to demonstrate it. (Martha Wilcox, 99)

Mrs. Eddy was no easier on her dressmaker, whom she expected to sew her dresses using only a dress form and without any fittings. Mrs. Wilcox defends this standard with the statement,

> Mrs. Eddy knew that Mind's work and Mind always fit—they are one and the same. And the sense of anything being too large or too small was not found in Mind. Therefore, excuses or alibis were of no avail with Mrs. Eddy. (Martha Wilcox, 95)

Mrs. Wilcox suggests that Mrs. Eddy was understanding if a sincere student failed to reach perfection in a particular endeavor, but she also states,

> Mrs. Eddy clearly discerned if one were striving to show forth God—his own right Mind—in everything. But if an

individual were not spiritually-minded enough to discern Mrs. Eddy's real purpose in these requirements, or thought them unnecessary, or thought Mrs. Eddy was just exacting and concerned only about the so-called material things, *or did not see the necessity of being obedient*—such a one did not remain long in the home. (Martha Wilcox, 95-96; emphasis added)

Mrs. Eddy also expected perfection from her workers when it came to "keeping watch" over her, protecting her from the attacks of malicious animal magnetism. Several of her students speak of these watches, which were usually two-hour segments during which the workers took turns mentally protecting Mrs. Eddy as she slept.[33] If she had a good night, she concluded that her students had kept their watches. If she had a bad night, she blamed her maladies on the students, no matter how diligently they had watched and "known the truth" over her during the night. Martha Wilcox describes a telling incident:

At one time, I was a mental worker for seven weeks. One evening she gave me a problem to work, and of course I had a great desire to prove the reality at hand, so worked the greater part of the night.

In the morning she called me to her and said, "Martha, why did you not do your work?" I replied, "Mother, I did." She said, "No, you didn't, you had a good talk with the devil. Why did you not know God's allness?"

I said, "Mother, I tried." And her reply was, "Well, if Jesus had just tried and failed, we would have no Science today." Then she had a card hung on the inside of the door to my room on which was printed in large letters, "Faith, without works, is dead." I looked at that for two weeks.[34]

There are many examples of both early and modern Christian Scientists living under doctrine over person and the demand for purity. This is inevitable in a religion which demands that its followers denounce their matter-based humanity and demonstrate their spiritual perfection. But the fact remains that we *are* human and we are *not* perfect. Many sincere believers have suffered greatly as they labored to reach the unattainable.

Notes

1 Barbara Wilson, *Blue Windows: A Christian Science Childhood* (New York: Picador USA, 1997), 153.

2 Mary Baker Eddy, *Science and Health with Key to the Scriptures* (Boston: Published by the Trustees under the Will of Mary Baker G. Eddy, 1934), 475.

3 Barbara Wilson, *Blue Windows: A Christian Science Childhood*, 158.

4 Ibid., 161.

5 Ibid., 159.

6 Robert J. Lifton, *Thought Reform and the Psychology of Totalism: A Study of "Brainwashing" in China* (1961; reprint, Chapel Hill: The University of North Carolina Press, 1989), 423-425, 430, 431.

7 Mary Baker Eddy, *Science and Health*, 401:27-402:7; Mary Baker Eddy, *The First Church of Christ Science and Miscellany* (Boston: Published by the Trustees under the Will of Mary Baker G. Eddy, 1941), 226:27-30.

8 Mary Baker Eddy, *Science and Health*, 464:13-19.

9

10 Ibid., 168:30-169:9, 401:7-20, 422:5-21.

11 Emma E. Newman, "The Primary Class of 1889 and Other Memories," *We Knew Mary Baker Eddy*, 1st series (Boston: The Christian Science Publishing Society, 1943), 25.

12 Caroline Fraser, Suffering Children and the Christian Science Church, *The Atlantic Monthly* (April 1995).

13 Peter Haldeman, "Growing Up Haldeman," (*New York Times*, 3 April 1994).

14 Mary Baker Eddy, *Rudimental Divine Science* (Boston: Published by the Trustees under the Will of Mary Baker G. Eddy, 1936), 16:15-16, 17:1.

15 Adam H. Dickey, *Memoirs of Mary Baker Eddy* (1927; reprint, Santa Clarita, CA: The Bookmark, n.d.), 27.

16 Barbara Wilson, *Blue Windows: A Christian Science Childhood*, 71, 72.

17 Suzanne Shepard, "Suffer the Little Children," *Redbook*, October 1994.

18 Private communication with Suzanne Shepard, 1998.

19 Rita Swan, "Children, Medicine, Religion, and the Law," in *Advances in Pediatrics* 44 (1997): 491-543; Caroline Fraser, "Suffering Children and the Christian Science Church,"

The Atlantic Monthly (April 1995); Rita Swan, "Cry, the Beloved children," (This and many other references are available from Children's Healthcare Is a Legal Duty, Inc., Box 2604, Sioux City, Iowa 51106); Suzanne Shepard, "Suffer the Little Children," *Redbook,* October 1994; Thomas Simmons, *The Unseen Shore: Memories of a Christian Science Childhood* (Boston: Beacon, 1991); Seth M. Asser and Rita Swan, "Child Fatalities from Religion-motivated Medical Neglect, *Pediatrics* 101, no. 4 (1998): 625-629.

20　The *Christian Science Journal* (April 1898), 15.

21　Robert Peel, *Mary Baker Eddy: The Years of Trial* (New York: Holt, Rinehart and Winston, 1971), 117.

22　Julia Bartlett, "A Worker in the Massachusetts Metaphysical College," *We Knew Mary Baker Eddy,* 4th series (Boston: The Christian Science Publishing Society, 1972), 68-69.

23　Willa Cather and Georgine Milmine, *The Life of Mary Baker G. Eddy & the History of Christian Science* (1909; reprint, Lincoln: University of Nebraska Press, 1993), 155.

24　Ibid., 297.

25　Mary Baker Eddy, *Science and Health,* 284:30-31.

26　Mary Baker Eddy, *Message to The Mother Church Boston, Massachusetts June, 1901* (Boston: Published by the Trustees under the Will of Mary Baker G. Eddy, 1929), 5:14-22.

27　Martha Wilcox, "A Worker in Mrs. Eddy's Chestnut Hill Home," *We Knew Mary Baker Eddy,* 4th series (Boston: The Christian Science Publishing Society, 1972), 89.

28　Martha Wilcox, *We Knew Mary Baker Eddy,* 4th series, 92.

29　Emma Newman, *We Knew Mary Baker Eddy,* 1st series, 35.

30　Martha Wilcox, *We Knew Mary Baker Eddy,* 4th series, 94.

31　Adam H. Dickey, *Memoirs of Mary Baker Eddy,* 23.

32　Martha Wilcox, *We Knew Mary Baker Eddy,* 4th series, 94, 95.

33　Adam Dickey describes the watches in his *Memoirs of Mary Baker Eddy,* 16-20.

34　Martha Wilcox, *We Knew Mary Baker Eddy,* 4th series, 99-100.

CHAPTER NINE
Ultimate Truth: The Sacred Science

The collective doctrines and teachings of a group constitute its "sacred science." These teachings are considered sacred because they emanate from an infallible source and cannot be disputed. They are believed to be a science because they are precise and provide answers to life's questions and problems. Both the sacred science and the leader who advocates it are above criticism.

The basics of Christian Science doctrine were described in Chapter Two. This doctrine constitutes a belief system; but can it be considered a sacred science? Some quotes from Mrs. Eddy and her followers should answer the question:

Statements from Mrs. Eddy:

> To mortal sense Christian Science seems abstract, but the process is simple and the results are sure if the Science is understood. . . . The Christian Scientist should understand and adhere strictly to the rules of divine metaphysics as laid down in this work, and rest his demonstration on this sure basis.[1]

> Science is absolute and final.[2]

You command the situation if you understand that mortal existence is a state of self-deception and not the truth of being.[3]

... man *is,* not *shall be,* perfect and immortal.[4]

If the student adheres strictly to the teachings of Christian Science and ventures not to break its rules, he cannot fail of success in healing.[5]

That evil or matter has neither intelligence nor power, is the doctrine of absolute Christian Science, and this is the great truth which strips all disguise from error.[6]

A Christian Scientist requires my work *Science and Health* for his textbook, and so do all his students and patients. Why? *First:* Because it is the voice of Truth to this age, and contains the full statement of Christian Science, or the Science of healing through Mind. *Second:* Because it was the first book known, containing a thorough statement of Christian Science. Hence it gave the first rules for demonstrating this Science, and registered the revealed Truth uncontaminated by human hypotheses. Other works, which have borrowed from this book without giving it credit, have adulterated the Science. *Third:* Because this book has done more for teacher and student, for healer and patient, than has been accomplished by other books.[7]

Jesus taught by the wayside, in humble homes. He spake of Truth and Love to artless listeners and dull disciples. His immortal words were articulated in a decaying language, and then left to the providence of God. Christian Science was to interpret them; and woman, "last at the cross," was to awaken the dull senses, intoxicated with pleasure or pain, to the infinite meaning of those words.[8]

If the student goes away to practice Truth's teachings only in part, dividing his interests between God and mammon and substituting his own views for Truth, he will inevitably reap the error he sows. Whoever would demonstrate the healing of Christian Science must abide strictly by its rules, heed every statement, and advance from the rudiments laid down. There is nothing difficult nor toilsome in this task, when the way is pointed out; but self-denial, sincerity, Christianity, and persistence alone win the prize, as they usually do in every department of life.[9]

... no matter how exalted a position a Christian Scientist may occupy at the moment, never accept what he may say as valid unless you can verify the statement in our textbook, *Science and Health with Key to the Scriptures.*[10]

Every By-Law in the [Mother Church] *Manual* is inspired. I did not write them any more than I wrote *Science and Health.* I study *Science and Health* constantly.[11]

No human pen nor tongue taught me the Science contained in this book, *Science and Health;* and neither tongue nor pen can overthrow it.[12]

In the words of St. John: "He shall give you another Comforter, that he may abide with you *forever.*" This Comforter I understand to be Divine [Christian] Science.[13]

Statements from Mrs. Eddy's Students:

One of her marked characteristics was that she rarely allowed anybody to criticize any of her writings, or call attention to what he considered an inappropriate expression. Even if there seemed good reason for a criticism, she was loath to accept it and in the majority of cases resisted what she considered to be interference from her critics. She wanted her book to be the product of her own thought and not a mixture of what mortal mind felt or believed on the subject. . . . Had she been any less wise than she was in her handling of this question, her book might indeed have presented much confused thought by reason of the interpolations of uninspired critics. (Adam Dickey)[14]

. . . she spoke of the absurdity of the literal translation of the Bible. Everything in the Bible, she told us, has its spiritual interpretation. . . . (Sue Harper Mims)[15]

. . . turning our thought to our Leader's other writings, when we seek the teaching contained in her *Prose Works,* is it not heart-warming to know that she is herself instructing us on practically every subject and situation in life, just as truly as though we sat in her classroom? (Daisette McKenzie)[16]

Through Mary Baker Eddy, God has given to humanity the complete, final revelation of Truth, divine Science. (Calvin Hill)[17]

Moses gave us the moral law. Elias exemplified prophecy. Christ Jesus demonstrated the divine law in the destruction of sin, disease, and death. Mrs. Eddy gave us the Science of Christianity which forever reveals to all mankind the practical application of the divine law in everyday experience. (Clara Knox McGee)[18]

The students . . . listened earnestly while our beloved Leader read to us these impressive words from *Science and Health* . . . "When we realize that there is but one Mind, the divine law of loving our neighbors as ourselves is unfolded to us; whereas a belief in many ruling minds hinders man's normal drift to-wards the one Mind, one God, and leads human thought into opposite channels, where selfishness reigns." . . . As she read this to us from our inspired textbook, *it seemed as if those few lines alone furnished the rule for working out every human problem,* no matter how difficult it might seem. . . . (Annie Knott, emphasis added)[19]

It should be clear that both Mrs. Eddy and her students believed that Christian Science was divinely inspired, infallible, and provided the solution to life's problems if its methods were applied correctly. Thus, Christian Science qualifies as a "sacred science" by Lifton's definition.

One might think that I have made my point using selected quotes from a few extra-zealous Christian Scientists. My response to this assumption is three-fold. First, the students' comments are consistent with Mrs. Eddy's views about Christian Science. Second, the students I am quoting were accomplished Christian Scientists; many were part of Mrs. Eddy's "inner circle" of followers. The Church authorized book, *Historical Sketches,* directs that we should believe statements made by this group of people:

Especially in the case of those who worked directly with Mrs. Eddy and shared many of her experiences, a special measure of respect and textual integrity is demanded. These are the workers she chose—individuals who served as her lieutenants, often for many years. To describe them as sturdy, strong-minded workers, patriarchal in their devotion and self-sacrifice, scarcely does them justice.[20]

My third point is that most of the quotes I have chosen are from authorized Christian Science literature. That means that they are portraying the Church's "official" image of Mrs. Eddy and her religion.

The other quotes I have chosen are also from Mrs. Eddy's most trusted students and have value based upon the above comment from *Historical Sketches.*

Notes

1 Mary Baker Eddy, *Science and Health with Key to the Scriptures* (Boston: Published by the Trustees under the Will of Mary Baker G. Eddy, 1934), 459:24-26, 31-32, 460:1-2.

2 Mary Baker Eddy, *Miscellaneous Writings, 1883-1896* (Boston: Published by the Trustees under the Will of Mary Baker G. Eddy, 1924), 99:1.

3 Mary Baker Eddy, *Science and Health,* 403:14-16.

4 Ibid., 428:22-23.

5 Ibid., 448:26-28.

6 Ibid., 454:11-13.

7 Ibid., 456:25-457:6.

8 Mary Baker Eddy, *Miscellaneous Writings,* 99:32-100:7.

9 Mary Baker Eddy, *Science and Health,* 462:9-19.

10 Abigail Dyer Thompson, "Loved Memories of Mary Baker Eddy," *We Knew Mary Baker Eddy,* 1st Series (Boston: The Christian Science Publishing Society, 1943), 69.

11 John Lathrop, "Reflections of Mary Baker Eddy," *We Knew Mary Baker Eddy,* 1st series (Boston: The Christian Science Publishing Society, 1943), 22.

12 Mary Baker Eddy, *Science and Health,* 110:17-20.

13 Ibid., 55:27-29.

14 Adam H. Dickey, *Memoirs of Mary Baker Eddy* (1927; reprint, Santa Clarita, CA: The Bookmark, n.d.), 34.

15 Sue Harper Mims, "An Intimate Picture of Our Leader's Final Class," *We Knew Mary Baker Eddy,* 2nd series (Boston: The Christian Science Publishing Society, 1950), 50.

16 Daisette D. S. McKenzie, "The Writings of Mary Baker Eddy," *We Knew Mary Baker Eddy,* 1st series (Boston: The Christian Science Publishing Society, 1943), 41.

17 Calvin Hill, "Some Precious Memories of Mary Baker Eddy," *We Knew Mary Baker Eddy,* 3rd series (Boston: The Christian Science Publishing Society, 1953), 58.

18 Clara Knox McKee, "With sandals off and staff in hand," *We Knew Mary Baker Eddy,* 2nd series (Boston: The Christian Science Publishing Society, 1950), 74.

19 Annie M. Knott, "Reminiscences of Mary Baker Eddy," *We Knew Mary Baker Eddy,* 3rd series (Boston: The Christian Science Publishing Society, 1953), 78-79.

20 Clifford P. Smith, *Historical Sketches from the Life of Mary Baker Eddy and the History of Christian Science* (Boston: The Christian Science Publishing Society, 1934, 1992), xii.

CHAPTER TEN
Words and Walls: Loading the Language

Loaded language: Redefined words, thought stopping clichés, complexity, and a special jargon—all of which support a group's "sacred science" and emotionally isolate its members from other points of view.

There is no greater lie than to change the meaning of a word while claiming to clarify it. To change the meaning of words in this manner is to lock one's listeners into a new language without their knowledge, effectively isolating them from the world.

"Loading the language" is a common technique used by those who desire to control the hearts and minds of others. There are several ways to change the meanings of words. One technique uses thought stopping clichés which produce instant emotion and prejudice within the minds of the deceived. For example, some mind-controlling groups refer to outsiders with names like "the unenlightened" or "Satan's emissaries." Such labels destroy the credibility of those nonmembers so that they are feared or not taken seriously when they point out the group's weaknesses.

Another way to load the language is to assign new meanings to common words. This effectively creates a new language that isolates group members from outsiders who try to talk with them about the group's beliefs or, as in the case of Christian Science, about reality itself. This technique is commonly used by religious groups whose leaders have written "divinely inspired" books to "explain" the Bible.

A third method for loading the language involves making its sentence structure so complex, rambling, or circular in logic that it is difficult to understand. The believer is told that he will understand it if he just keeps studying. He is led to believe that his inability to grasp the meaning of the writings is due to his own shortcomings, and not to problems with the text itself.

All of these techniques form an invisible barrier between the deceived and the world around him. A group member and an outsider can think they are having a meaningful conversation and not even realize that they are speaking about completely different subjects.

Mrs. Eddy was a master at loading language. She changed the meaning of many secular words and of almost every biblical term considered central to Christianity. She convinced her followers that these changes represented enlightenment rather than new definitions, and taught that Christian Scientists were the only people with the "truth" (thus, labeling "non-Scientists" as "the unenlightened" without directly saying so). She turned the English language upside down, making "substance" a term referring only to spiritual things[1] and classifying matter as unreal. She described seven synonyms for God (Principle, Mind, Soul, Spirit, Life, Truth, and Love), and then used these words to define each other.

Mrs. Eddy created a glossary in *Science and Health* in order to define many of the terms central to her doctrine.[2] Consider these examples:

MOTHER. God; divine and eternal Principle; Life, Truth, Love (592:16-17).

RESURRECTION. Spiritualization of thought; a new and higher idea of immortality, or spiritual existence; material belief yielding to spiritual understanding (593:9-11).

> EYES. Spiritual discernment,—not material but mental (586:3-4).

As she reinterpreted these common words to fit her doctrine, Mrs. Eddy not only changed their meanings but also removed them from the realm of materiality. "Mother" no longer refers to a person but to God. Resurrection has nothing to do with rising from the dead but deals strictly with the spiritualization of one's thought. Eyes are definitely not material (then why do so many Christian Scientists wear glasses?). Barbara Wilson eloquently describes Mrs. Eddy's words with her comment, "Mrs. Eddy's language . . . was like cotton candy that vanished in your mouth as soon as you took a bite; . . . the words in *Science and Health* weren't proper words, they were metaphysical concepts, abstractions with no teeth, no elbows or legs."[3]

Nenneman addresses Mrs. Eddy's use of words in some detail, stating that she threw an "entirely new light" on "familiar Christian terminology."[4] Von Fettweis and Warneck are more direct in their assessment, admitting that Christian Science language "contradicted" a number of traditional doctrines.[5]

Nenneman dedicates an entire chapter to the subject of terminology. His chapter is helpful to the uninitiated but underscores how differently Christian Scientists and non-Christian Scientists interpret the English language. For example, Mrs. Eddy differentiates between the human mind and the human consciousness, the former referring to an "unregenerate" mind and the latter describing a mind that has been "touched by Christ."[6] This and other subtle differences in the language can really cloud conversations between Christian Scientists and uninformed outsiders.

Mrs. Eddy was a master at complexity and circular logic. One of my favorite examples of her logic appears in *Science and Health,* where she makes the following statement as part of a "platform" meant to demonstrate the infallibility of divine metaphysics (remember that "Life, Truth, Love, Spirit, Principle, and Mind" are all synonyms for God as defined in the Glossary of *Science and Health*[7]):

God is what the Scriptures declare Him to be—Life, Truth, Love. Spirit is divine Principle, and divine Principle is Love, and Love is Mind, and Mind is not both good and bad, for God is Mind; therefore there is in reality one Mind only, because there is one God.[8]

Mrs. Eddy's students have picked up on her talent for linguistic gymnastics. I found this gem in the question and answer section of the October, 1890, *Christian Science Journal:*[9]

Question: When a person is cured of an old belief, is it Scientific to say that he is healed—or would it be more Scientific to say that persons are never healed? [Since the false belief was never real in the first place]. If the latter be correct, why does the *Journal* make statements about "healing?" Answer: This correspondent has himself, if he will note it, answered [the question]. His query is made in the seemings of belief about these seemings. The *Journal,* also, is printed in the seemings. When the sense of these seemings shall have been destroyed, cases, questions, and their foundation of seeming facts will all vanish together. No way of dealing with seemings in terms of absolute Science has yet been found.

This little gem illustrates the problem of using loaded language to straddle two states of existence. How can you heal something that was never really there, and then talk about it without "giving" it the reality that you had to deny in order to heal it in the first place? This straddling of the "absolute and the relative" goes right along with Mrs. Eddy's statement that she was never born,[10] is no longer here,[11] and that she had discovered what *did but did not* produce a certain problem regarding one of her book publications.[12] The day before she turned seventy-five years old she wrote, "tomorrow is my birthday. So saith mortal mind."[13] In other words she was saying, "tomorrow *is but is not* my birthday."

I remember discussing Christianity with friends when I was still a Christian Scientist. Although we had obvious doctrinal differences, it appeared that there were some basic principles on which we could agree. For example, we could all say that Jesus died for our sins. What I did not realize is that the phrase held completely different meanings for us. My friends were saying that Jesus died to *pay* for our sins, while I was saying that He died (to human belief) to prove that sin, disease, and death are unreal. My friends meant that Jesus was sacrificed on the cross to repair a breach in our relationship with God, while I meant that Jesus had gone to the cross to prove that a breach had never existed. We gave completely different interpretations to the phrase "Jesus died for our sins," but I thought that we were in basic agreement. How could this happen? The answer is simple—my friends and I were assigning different meanings to the words we used to interpret the phrase. We were using different definitions for God, Jesus, matter, death, sin, heaven, and hell. We could use the same phrase, but in a practical sense we were speaking different languages. After I left Christian Science I was surprised to discover that my friends and I had agreed on almost nothing. To further examine biblical issues, see the section entitled Christian Science and the Bible.

Much of *Science and Health* makes sense as long as one accepts the paradigm that matter is unreal. The writing can be quite complex even within that paradigm. To the Christian Scientist, this complexity seems utterly profound. To the former Christian Scientist, it seems like utter nonsense.

Notes

1 Mary Baker Eddy, *Science and Health with Key to the Scriptures* (Boston: Published by the Trustees under the Will of Mary Baker G. Eddy, 1934), 468:16-24.

2 Ibid., 579-599.

3 Barbara Wilson, *Blue Windows, A Christian Science Childhood* (New York: Picador USA, 1977), 48.

4 Richard A. Nenneman, *Persistent Pilgrim: The Life of Mary Baker Eddy* (Etna, NH: Nebbadoon Press, 1997), 193.

5 Yvonne Caché von Fettweis and Robert Townsend Warneck, *Mary Baker Eddy: Christian Healer* (Boston: The Christian Science Publishing Society, 1998), 113.

6   Richard A Nenneman, *Persistent Pilgrim: The Life of Mary Baker Eddy*, 263-271.

7   Mary Baker Eddy, *Science and Health*, 587:5-8.

8   Ibid., 330:19-24.

9   *Christian Science Journal* 8, no. 7 (1890): 308.

10   Annie, M. Knott, "Reminiscences of Mary Baker Eddy," *We Knew Mary Baker Eddy,* 3rd series (Boston: The Christian Science Publishing Society, 1953), 80-81.

11   Mary Baker Eddy, *The First Church of Christ Scientist and Miscellany* (Boston: Published by the Trustees under the Will of Mary Baker G. Eddy, 1941), 119:26-32.

12   Willa Cather & Georgine Milmine, *The Life of Mary Baker G. Eddy & the History of Christian Science* (1909; reprint, Lincoln: University of Nebraska Press, 1993), 394.

13   Richard A. Nenneman, *Persistent Pilgrim: The Life of Mary Baker Eddy*, 254.

CHAPTER ELEVEN
The Dispensing of Existence

The group fosters an attitude of superiority, labeling outsiders as unenlightened, damned, evil, and the like. Members are often afraid to leave the group because they are taught that to leave is to risk failure, damnation, shunning, or other serious consequences.

Lifton describes the "dispensing of existence" as a group's attitude about who has the right to exist. In other words, the group thinks that it possesses absolute truth and can decide who is "good" or "enlightened" and who is "bad" or "unenlightened." Although the term "right to exist" is usually taken figuratively, a few groups actually feel justified in killing nonmembers.

An elitist attitude makes members feel special and strengthens their loyalty to the group and its teachings. This same elitism makes members dependent upon the group. They are afraid to leave lest they lose the truth, find themselves unable to function without it, or face shunning by the people they love. Worse than that, they are often taught that abandoning their beliefs will produce frightening ramifications such as illness, death, or damnation.

When introduced to Lifton's model for mind control, my initial reaction was that Christian Scientists could not possibly practice the "dispensing of existence." "Most of them are very nice people," I thought. "They do not think of unbelievers as bad—just as temporarily unenlightened. After all, Christian Scientists believe that, either here or hereafter, everyone will eventually become a Christian Scientist. Could this attitude be elitism? If it is elitism, so what? What is wrong with believing that you are right?" Then I began to think about the subtle consequences of believing that Christian Science provides the only pathway to ultimate truth.

First, I began to realize that the Christian Scientist's attitude of loving condescension ("That's okay, dear—you just don't understand Christian Science") is not so loving after all. This attitude makes it difficult to admit to health problems or to leave the religion; lingering physical problems or defection represent failure. I left Christian Science because I was absolutely sure that it contradicted the Bible, but something inside me kept saying, "you're leaving the 'graduate school' of Christianity and going back to 'kindergarten.' " That is (in essence), what I had been taught to think about other defectors, and I could sense the same attitude being applied to me. I felt both humiliation and self-condemnation even though I believed that what I was doing was right.

A second and more unfortunate aspect of Christian Science elitism involves healing. When illness or injury lingers, a caregiver may become frightened or frustrated by the patient's lack of progress. The caregiver's attitude often changes from, "that's okay, you just don't understand," to "what's wrong with you? Why don't you understand?" Matters are often worse if the patient has rejected Christian Science, since the caregiver consciously or unconsciously blames the patient for not even trying to get better. After all, the person would not be sick and burdensome if he or she would just accept the Truth and be healed! The caregiver's concern or anger often emerge in the form of insensitive remarks, impatience, or worse. Too many children and adults have been punished, neglected, and abused because their healings did not come quickly enough to meet the spiritual and emotional needs of their well-meaning caregivers.

"All right, I thought. Christian Scientists are nice people who sometimes hurt themselves and others because of their elitist attitudes. But elitism, in itself, does not make Christian Science a mind-controlling religion." So I began to ponder the other elements of Lifton's "dispensing of existence." At first, I could not think of any scare tactics or shunning in my own experience.

Then I began to remember how I had subtly, but repeatedly, been warned about leaving the religion and opening myself up to mortal mind. I also remembered some of Mrs. Eddy's statements about leaving and about trying to practice one's own version of Christian Science. Then I began talking to people who *had* been shunned, either subtly or overtly. I kept digging, remembering, and asking questions. To my surprise and dismay, I found that Christian Science does fit Lifton's "dispensing of existence."

First, consider the issues of dependency and safety. Mrs. Eddy offered her followers "absolute truth" by presenting Christian Science as a divinely inspired, scientifically sure method for overcoming sickness and other "claims" of mortal mind. Then she emphasized the doctrine of animal magnetism, that illusion that is powerless but can prove deadly unless combated by the truth as revealed by her teachings. The implication is that one is safe only as long as he or she stays within the mental confines of Christian Science. I heard many times that leaving Christian Science would render me vulnerable to the claims of mortal mind and that dire consequences would eventually drive me back to Christian Science. I have heard several former Christian Scientists comment that they were afraid that something terrible would happen to them when they left the religion.

Did Mrs. Eddy foster this belief that life is unsafe outside of Christian Science? Of course she did. She taught that man will suffer from the belief in a material existence until he overcomes the belief. Overcoming the belief requires learning and practicing Christian Science *without* alteration. Add to this logic her comment in *Science and Health:*

Alas for those who break faith with divine Science and fail to strangle the serpent of sin as well as of sickness! They are dwellers still in the deep darkness of belief. They are in the surging sea of error, not struggling to lift their heads above the drowning wave.

What must the end be? They must eventually expiate their sin through suffering. The sin, which one has made his bosom companion, comes back to him at last with accelerated force, for the devil [speaking figuratively, since Christian Scientists do not believe in a real devil] knoweth his time is short. Here [Rev. 12:10-12] the Scriptures declare that evil is temporal, not eternal. The dragon is at last stung to death by his own malice; but how many periods of torture it may take to remove all sin, must depend upon sin's obduracy.[1]

In this passage Mrs. Eddy emphasizes that we all suffer from the beliefs of sin and disease until we abandon them and learn our true spiritual identity as taught by Christian Science. Death does not excuse us from learning this lesson. We will continue to suffer in the next plane of existence (consciousness), as well as on subsequent planes, until we forsake our belief in a material existence and are "saved." Mrs. Eddy's implication is that one is much better off if he studies Christian Science on this plane of existence than if he puts off the inevitable lessons until a later date. Consider another of her warnings against wandering from truth:

Animal magnetism, in its ascending steps of evil, entices its victim by unseen, silent arguments. Reversing the modes of good, in their silent allurements to health and holiness, it impels mortal mind into error of thought, and tempts into the committal of acts foreign to the natural inclinations. The victims lose their individuality, and lend themselves as willing tools to carry out the designs of their worst enemies, even those who would induce their self-destruction. Animal magnetism fosters suspicious distrust where honor is due, fear where courage should be strongest, reliance where there should be avoidance, a belief in safety where there is most danger; and these miserable lies, poured constantly into his mind, fret and confuse it, spoiling that individual's disposition, undermining his health, and sealing his doom, unless the cause of the mischief is found out and destroyed.

. . . animal magnetism is the highest form of mental evil, wherewith to complete the sum total of sin.

The question is often asked, Why is there so much dissension among mental practitioners? We answer, Because they do not practice in strict accordance with the teaching of Christian Science Mind-healing. . . .

Unless one's eyes are opened to the modes of mental malpractice, working so subtly that we mistake its suggestions for the impulses of our own thought, the victim will allow himself to drift in the wrong direction without knowing it. Be ever on guard against this enemy. Watch your thoughts, and see whether they lead you to God and into harmony with His true followers.[2]

The only way to defeat the terrible non-powers of animal magnetism and malpractice is to know their unreality—as taught by Christian Science.

The dispensing of existence often fosters an "us versus them" attitude. Christian Scientists usually seem like such loving people that this attitude is difficult to imagine. Mrs. Eddy, nevertheless, felt that people were either for her or against her. "Whoever is not for me is against me,"[3] she declared to Daniel Spofford as he fell from favor and joined the series of favorites she later denounced as mesmerists. She labeled Spofford as immoral (her term for disloyalty to Christian Science), and published her accusation in the local newspaper.[4] She also had a term for disaffected students who taught their own versions of Christian Science—she called them "aliens."[5]

The Board of Directors (which currently runs the Church) has perpetuated Mrs. Eddy's "for us or against us" attitude. One example of this disposition can be found in the so-called Great Litigation (1919-1921), a power struggle between the Board of Directors and the Trustees of the Publishing Society. The conflict found its way to the Supreme Court of Massachusetts, where the court ruled in favor of the directors. During the struggle, the directors attempted to bankrupt the Publishing Society by asking loyal church members to cancel their subscriptions to the Christian Science periodicals. Before long, church-goers who continued their subscriptions were labeled as disloyal and were shunned by members who had cancelled their subscriptions. After the litigation ended, the directors sent a questionnaire to all practitioners who wanted to be listed in the *Christian Science Journal* (in other words, to be recognized by the Church). The questionnaire required the practitioners to disclose their loyalties regarding the Great Litigation—a clear misuse of the directors' power since they were the ones deciding which practitioners would be listed in the *Christian Science Journal.*[6]

According to the Christian Science Foundation (a group of modern-day Christian Scientists who are drawing attention to alleged abuses within the Church leadership), many sincere Christian Scientists have resigned from the Church or have been excommunicated because of the directors' policies regarding what church members can read and think. The Christian Science Foundation describes the Christian Science Church as requiring "unquestioning obedience," an interesting term for this discussion of mind control.[7]

The Christian Science Foundation is one of a growing number of organizations founded by Christian Scientists who disagree with how the Board of Directors is running the Church. Interestingly, these devout Christian Scientists are known as "dissidents."[8] I have not searched for examples, but I know several former Christian Scientists who feel that their character, mental state, and/or professional standards have been maligned by the Church when they presented testimony or information that the Church perceived as threatening. Apparently, the church leadership's "us versus them" attitude includes anyone who opposes it, either from without or from within.

Most individual Christian Scientists do not hold the "us versus them" attitude as strongly as their leader or the Board of Directors—except in the area of medical care. When an outsider mentions a failed healing to a Christian Scientist, the Christian Scientist usually counters with a story about the failings of medicine as if the shortcomings of medicine somehow validate Christian Science. With the Christian Science disdain for medicine, many Christian Scientists are actually afraid of seeing a doctor. Mrs. Eddy emphasized the "medicine is bad" attitude in her address to a convention of the National Christian Scientist Association in 1888. The essence of her speech is preserved in *Miscellaneous Writings,* and at the end she states:

> Christian Science and Christian Scientists will, *must,* have a history; and if I could write the history in poor parody on Tennyson's grand verse, it would read thus:
>
> Traitors to right of them,
> M.D.'s to left of them,
> Priestcraft in front of them,
> Volleyed and thundered!
> Into the jaws of hate,
> Out through the door of Love,
> On to the blest above,
> Marched the one hundred.[9]

Notice how the doctors are nicely sandwiched between the traitors and the jaws of hate. It is not surprising that a trip to the doctor can produce fear and feelings of disloyalty in the sincere Christian Scientist.

With the focus on elitism, fear, and judgmental attitudes, it is easy to forget that Christian Scientists practice the ultimate "dispensing of existence"—they reject their own bodies and, indeed, any form of material existence. When they are thinking "scientifically," everything they see, hear, taste, feel, and touch must be spiritualized into something else.

Notes

1 Mary Baker Eddy, *Science and Health with Key to the Scriptures* (Boston: Published by the Trustees under the Will of Mary Baker G. Eddy, 1934), 569:14-28.

2 Mary Baker Eddy, *The First Church of Christ Scientist and Miscellany* (Boston: Published by the Trustees under the Will of Mary Baker G. Eddy, 1941), 211:12-28, 212:12-17, 213:15-21.

3 Willa Cather and Georgine Milmine, *The Life of Mary Baker G. Eddy & the History of Christian Science* (1909; reprint, Lincoln: University of Nebraska Press, 1993), 234.

4 Ibid., 233-234.

5 Yvonne Caché von Fettweis and Robert Townsend Warneck, *Mary Baker Eddy: Christian Healer* (Boston: The Christian Science Publishing Society, 1998), 119.

6 "The Continuity of the Cause of Christian Science," in a compendium published by the Christian Science Foundation, Box 440, Cambridge CB4 3BH, England, 1992, 1995, 11:3-11:8.

7 Ibid., 11:7.

8 A few of the dissident organizations include: The Banner, 2040 Hazel Ave., Zanesville, OH 43701; The Bookmark, Box 801143, Santa Clarita, CA 91380; The Christian Science Foundation (see above endnote). These organizations support both Mrs. Eddy and Christian Science, but are labeled dissident because they dare to question The Mother Church's leadership (i.e., the Board of Directors) and/or to publish books not authorized by the Christian Science Publishing Society. "That they may all be one" is a video tape in which several loyal and well-known Christian Scientists express concern about current Church leadership and tell why they finally decided to speak out about it. Both the tape and a collection letters commenting on it (called "A sharing of responses to the video 'That they all may be one' ") refer to "dissidents" as if the term is widely known within the Christian Science community. The tape and letters (1995) can be obtained at Box 627, Natick, MA 01760-0006.

9 Mary Baker Eddy, *Miscellaneous Writings*, 1883-1896 (Boston: Published by the Trustees under the Will of Mary Baker G. Eddy, 1924), 106:3-14.

CHAPTER TWELVE
Calling the Question

By now it should be clear that Christian Science is not as liberating as it initially appears. Its followers emphasize spiritual dominion and healing while many among their ranks suffer with fear and guilt, quietly struggling with problems they cannot heal. They quote Mrs. Eddy's statement, "the time for thinkers has come,"[1] even as they allow her to shape their view of reality. Does Christian Science involve mind control? Yes. Is it a cult in the psychological sense? Yes. It does not control what its people eat, where they live, or whom they marry, but it controls their worldview and greatly influences their actions and emotional well-being. Its damage is hard to identify because it is usually hidden behind smiles and denial.

The Church's membership has been in decline for several years.[2] Although actual membership figures are a closely guarded secret, the trend is obvious based upon the number of churches closing and from the declining number of practitioners listed in the *Christian Science Journal*. If Christian Science may die a natural death, why bother to publish a book exposing its mind controlling nature? There are good reasons for expending the effort.

First, Christian Science is trying very hard *not* to expire. Through mass marketing techniques and, for the first time in my memory, active recruitment, it is attempting to gain new members and blend into mainstream religion and society. The following developments illustrate the point.

Science and Health was recently published in a modern-style trade edition. After its publication, I was surprised to see the book in major bookstores and to notice bookmarks advertising *Science and Health* at checkout counters. According to a 1998 article in *Christianity Today,* the book sold over 100,000 copies annually from 1993 through 1997.[3]

The Church is promoting *Science and Health* as a self-help book rather than as religious literature. A friend recently heard the book advertised on the radio, and Christian Science was never mentioned. Considering *Science and Health's* status as the "Christian Science textbook," it is deceptive to advertise the book without mentioning its religious connections.

The Church is capitalizing on society's recent interest in alternative healing methods, including prayer. In 1997, the head of the Church's Board of Directors told *Christianity Today,* "nary a day goes by that I don't hear from a minister or a doctor that says they're using [*Science and Health*]."[4] This recent development is amazing considering Christianity's historical view of Christian Science and the Christian Science disdain for medicine.

The Church has recently embarked upon a multi-million dollar renovation project at The Mother Church in Boston. Principia College recently completed a major renovation and building project which would suggest that the school's enrollment is growing rather than declining (the enrollment is significantly less than when I attended during the late 1970s). These projects are consistent with a religious group that wants to appear healthy and innovative.

The Christian Science periodicals have been re-designed to improve their public appeal. For example, the weekly *Christian Science Sentinel* has been enlarged to look like other magazines; its cover is in full color and looks like any other modern, spiritually oriented "self-help" magazine, and the letters in the word "Sentinel" are six times larger than the letters in "Christian Science," de-emphasizing the specific denomination involved in its publication. The magazine is filled with color photographs and articles about popular subjects—the millennium, fitness, ethics, self-esteem, and public safety. The back cover has a full-page ad for *Science and Health* with the statement, "For People Who Aren't Afraid To Think." Most surprisingly, the *Sentinel* contains an "items of interest" section quoting inspirational tidbits from a host of secular and religious sources, including popular stars such as talk show host Oprah Winfrey.[5] This is not the rather formal *Sentinel* I remember and is clearly designed to attract the modern religious crowd.

The Church maintains a web site offering current information about its activities and basic information about Christian Science. It also provides on-line audio lectures on Christian Science, as well as information regarding its radio broadcasts, short wave radio broadcasts, and publications. The web site makes Christian Science easily accessible on a global scale.

The developments described above suggest that people are still being lured into Christian Science, even as others leave the religion. These potential converts need to understand the dangers of Christian Science so they can balance them against the Church's utopian promises.

A second reason to expose the damaging nature of Christian Science is that tens of thousands of people have been affected by this religion. An alarming number of these people remain hurting and confused. Their experiences and wounds often begin to make sense when viewed in light of mind control theory.

Because of recent scandals within the church leadership, many disillusioned believers have left the Church but have remained Christian Scientists. Will they fare better than those who remain under the Church's authority? Perhaps, but probably not much better. I say this because the heart of Christian Science mind control lies in Mrs. Eddy's writings and not in the current Church leadership. The independent Christian Scientist may face less peer pressure, but he or she still faces the internal pressures and controls built into Christian Science doctrine. Mrs. Eddy is still the leader if one is truly a Christian Scientist.

I know many people who claim to practice their own version of Christian Science. They keep the utopian promises while mixing in some other philosophies or a little medicine. To these people I say, you are welcome to believe anything you wish, but don't claim to have your own version of Christian Science. Mrs. Eddy made it very clear that Christian Science is absolute truth and that it must be practiced without alteration. Believe as you please, but don't call your eclectic beliefs Christian Science. Incidentally, I have noticed that practicing one's own version of Christian Science does not necessarily protect one from emotional damage; it just avoids much of the guilt.

Most of the Christian Scientists I know love their God and are sincere in their quest for truth. But I have met people from a host of cults and can say the same thing about them. To all of these people, I quote Mrs. Eddy's statement, "the time for thinkers has come." Think about the evidence presented in this book. Look within yourself without spiritualizing away your physical senses and true emotions. Are you truly free?

I will end this discussion by again quoting Barbara Wilson:

> To have a body—I knew this deeply, without thinking—was to touch and taste and smell your way through a world that was endlessly rich and varied.[6]

To quote another former Christian Scientist, "It's nice to be real."

Notes

1 Mary Baker Eddy, *Science and Health with Key to the Scriptures* (Boston: Published by the Trustees under the Will of Mary Baker G. Eddy 1934), vii:13.

2 Rodney Stark. 1998. "The Rise and Fall of Christian Science," *Journal of Contemporary Religion* 13 (2): 189-214.

3 Mark A Kellner. 1998. Christian Science Aims to Shine Tarnished Image. *Christianity Today*, October, 28. (Article taken from the magazine's *Christianity Online* at http://www.christianity.net.

4 Ibid.

5 The article subjects are taken from the 4 January 1999 and 1 February 1999 editions of the *Christian Science Sentinel*. Oprah Winfrey is quoted in the 1 February edition, 5.

6 Barbara Wilson, *Blue Windows: A Christian Science Childhood* (New York: Picador USA, 1997), 71.

Epilogue

Some who read this book will thank me for writing it, telling me that I have validated their experiences and given words to their pain. Other readers will accuse me of intolerance. Devout Christian Scientists will tell me that I just don't understand.

Someone will surely point out Mrs. Eddy's 1872 statement:

> The idea that expresses moral [Christian] science is physical, and we see this idea traced out in one continuous page of nature's bright and glorious character. Every blade of grass, tree and flower, declare, "How manifold are thy works, O Lord! in wisdom hast thou made them all.¹"

The person who shows me this statement may quote Richard Nenneman's description of the:

> intellectual sticking point for thousands . . . who . . . turn to Christian Science . . . without the spiritual openness required to gain the meaning of her words. Matter [is] unreal, yes; but basing one's thought on the perfect spiritual creation of God [does] not take away one iota of what [is] good in human experience. Yet looking only at statements of absolute spiritual fact, without their application to the present human experience, might easily lead anyone into an intellectual dead end.²

Believe it or not, I do understand the above statements regarding what Christian Scientists call the Absolute and the Relative. When I was a

Christian Scientist I *did* appreciate the beauty of Creation as well as other positive aspects of human experience. That does not change the fact that I had to spiritually interpret them and deny the negative aspects of my human experience. And let us not forget Mrs. Eddy's statements, sprinkled throughout this book, which undermine even the *positive* human experience when the human body is involved. Christian Science somehow disconnected me from myself, and I have seen it do the same to others.

I did not leave Christian Science out of anger or disillusionment, but because of doctrinal problems I could not ignore. It took months of Bible study to get me out of Christian Science. It took *years* to get Christian Science out of me. My childhood beliefs and loyalties were so deeply ingrained that something inside me refused let go. I did not find emotional freedom and resolution until I began to examine Christian Science in light of mind control and to compare Mrs. Eddy's practices with those of other cult leaders.

I have not written this book out of resentment or in an attempt to retaliate against the Church. I have written it out of a sincere desire to help those who need to hear its message. I have shared this information with enough grateful people to know that my message is relevant. I hope it has been helpful to you.

Notes

1   Richard A. Nenneman, *Persistent Pilgrim: The Life of Mary Baker Eddy* (Etna, NH: Nebbadoon Press, 1997), 117.

2   Ibid., 117-118.

My Story: A Journey to Freedom

A Glimmer of Truth

I never wanted to leave Christian Science. I spent the first 30 years of my life believing that this religion represented the highest form of truth. Christian Science taught me that God's creation is spiritual and not material. It promised that as I understood this fact and its natural conclusion that sin, disease, and death are unreal, my experience would reflect this understanding. I would be able to heal my illnesses and conquer any problems that "seemed" to come my way. What a wonderful promise! It gave me an "overcoming" attitude which carried me through the many ups and downs of life.

I grew up in a family of Christian Scientists. My mother's parents converted when she was very young, and my father joined Christian Science as a young adult. My sister and I both attended and loved Principia College, a school for Christian Scientists. I then became very active in the student group at my graduate school. I married a "non-Scientist" who was willing to attend church with me. We attended a Christian Science church during the first several years of our marriage, although I never formally joined that local church (I was, however, a member of The Mother Church.)

I believed, with all my heart, that Christian Science was the truth. Yet, there was one aspect of my religious life that troubled me. I was dissatisfied with my success as a healer. Healing is greatly emphasized in this religion, both because it is said to validate the religious doctrine and because it indicates the spiritual maturity of the believer. The system has supposedly been validated by "thousands of healings," so a Christian Scientist's failure to heal a problem is said to reflect his own lack of understanding rather than to reveal a problem with the system. I felt inadequate as a healer even though I had experienced a few healings during my life and had heard of many others (real or imagined). I became very concerned about this "inadequacy" after the birth of my first child. Parents are responsible for healing their young children—I knew that, for the safety of my child, I needed to become a more consistent healer.

Frankly, I was getting a little bored with the study format set up by the Church. I decided to set *Science and Health* aside for a time and to confine my study to the Bible. I reasoned that since Mrs. Eddy's writings were based on the Bible, focusing on it for a while should help me better understand her writings and should ultimately make me a better healer. I had a deep need to understand the truth and was open to anything that God's Word had to offer. I prayed for the truth and began my journey.

I am convinced that many of God's miracles involve the timing of events in our lives. God brought a Christian family into my life about the time that I began my search. I felt a special love for these people and offered Christian Science to them as an answer to long-standing health problems. This opened up a conversation during which we shared our beliefs. They talked about the themes central to Christianity, such as Jesus' sacrificial death on the cross and our need to accept that sacrifice in a personal way in order to reap its benefits. I appreciated their love for Jesus and their devotion to God, but the things they said about salvation, heaven, hell, and the like seemed naïve and ridiculous to me. I had been taught that non-Christian Scientists had an incomplete understanding of Jesus' true message, and our conversation seemed to confirm this belief.

I kept reading the Bible, beginning with the Gospels. Several months later I asked my friends if we could have another discussion about Christian beliefs. In my mind there were Christian Scientists, and "everybody else." I had no concept of the vast differences between the many Christian denominations and simply wanted a better understanding of what the rest of the Christian world believed. This gave my friends a second opportunity to explain their beliefs to me. Again, what they said sounded terribly naïve. They just told me to keep reading.

I entered the book of Romans on July 6, 1985. I was using the King James Version of the Bible, and Paul's writings became very confusing in "the King's English." I switched to a modern English version, and the text became a little easier to follow. When I reached the third chapter I encountered a passage that I had never seen before:

> . . . for all have sinned and fall short of the glory of God, and are justified freely by his grace through the redemption that came by Christ Jesus. God presented him as a sacrifice of atonement,[1] through faith in his blood. (Rom. 3:23-25a, NIV)

Everything my friends had said seemed to be wrapped up in that one passage. I suddenly realized that Jesus had not gone to the cross to prove the unreality of sin, disease, and death, but to *pay* for my sins, "for *all* have sinned." The things my friends had said suddenly didn't seem so naïve. I caught a glimmer of truth, and my life has never been the same.

I can't believe the change that occurred in me. It wasn't a bolt of lightning—it was a steady and very definite change in my values and beliefs. I had been raised with a solid set of Judeo-Christian values and held high moral standards. I was intrigued, therefore, to find that my attitudes and values seemed to be "fine-tuned" over the next several weeks. I was frequently surprised to find myself thinking, "I didn't know that I felt quite that way" about some issue regarding integrity, morality, and the like. These weren't major shifts, but they were definitely changes that were happening without my conscious input or any influence from those around me. God was definitely working on me. It was a spiritually rich and exciting time as the Bible came to life, teaching me things that I had never known even though I had read it all of my life. I was tremendously excited. At the same time I faced a serious problem: Christian Science claimed to elucidate the Bible, but its teachings suddenly seemed to contradict it. I went through a six-week period of intense Bible study in order to settle this dilemma. One by one, the basic doctrines of Christianity loomed before me—doctrines such as the reality of heaven and hell, the identity of the Holy Spirit, the purpose for Jesus' crucifixion, and Jesus' true identity. I fought the issues one at a time, trying to make Christian Science fit with the Bible. Each time I discovered that in spiritualizing a biblical term, Mrs. Eddy had actually redefined the term. I knew that Mrs. Eddy's spiritualized meanings would clarify, rather than disagree, with the original biblical concepts if she had truly received them from God. Finally, I had to concede that Christian Science contradicts the Bible rather than elucidating it. I had no choice but to leave Christian Science.

One would think that leaving Christian Science would be easy after discovering that its doctrine is flawed. Many people do leave the religion without looking back. In some cases, they even forget what Christian Science taught them as God replaces it with His unadulterated truth from the Bible. But Christian Science is more than a set of doctrinal beliefs—it is a different view of reality. It teaches that the material world is unreal and makes its followers live in a state of almost constant denial as they reinterpret reality in order to heal their problems. This denial can result in terrible physical, emotional, and spiritual damage. I have observed this damage over and over in the lives of both current and former Christian Scientists.

I know former Christian Scientists who fall all along the spectrum I have just described. While some seem healthy, many others suffer fallout which requires prayer, spiritual growth, a lot of forgiveness, and sometimes counseling in order to be healed. Others carry emotional scars for a lifetime without understanding their connection to Christian Science. In my case, I fought a long battle to break free from the emotional hold this religion had on me and to deal with the scars it had left in my life.

Hearing about my journey toward wholeness has sometimes been helpful to former Christian Scientists as it has enabled them to finally put their undefined hurts and impressions into words. My story has also helped non-Christian Scientists better understand the struggles and sometimes odd behavior of Christian Science loved ones, who suffer needlessly with treatable physical and emotional problems and yet refuse to handle them medically.

I tell my story out of a deep love and concern for Christian Scientists.

The Journey to Freedom

As I said before, I did not want to leave Christian Science. All of my life I had been taught that this religion was the highest form of truth. I felt a tremendous sense of loss as I left the only religion I had ever known. My identity was built around Christian Science. It had formed the basis for my world view (matter is an illusion—all is spiritual). As a Navy family, my family moved many times during my childhood, and the uniformity of Christian Science churches and their people had added an element of stability to the exciting, but rather destabilizing, lifestyle the Navy had imposed upon me. When I entered Principia College, I found friends from all over the country. I also found a whole group of people who held my rather unorthodox view of reality. I felt at home and spiritually normal, and immediately sank my roots deep into Principia.

Leaving Christian Science meant disappointing my parents, losing the spiritual link to much of my family and closest friends, and losing the college roots that I held so dear. Despite the wonderful things happening in my life, there was a part of me that felt terribly alone.

On top of that, I was sick. As a wife, mother, and Ph.D. chemist with a career, I was already operating at peak physical capacity when I found Christ. Then I started my Bible study. The only time to do this work was after my family went to bed. I studied for hours at a time, sleeping very little for several weeks. I lacked the physical reserves to operate this way and began to pay a physical toll. I had experienced some near-fainting spells even before finding Christ (which I now know were related to my eating habits coupled with my happy, but stressful lifestyle), so decided to see a doctor. I thought I might have diabetes. I was given a series of incorrect diagnoses and treatments that only exacerbated the problem, partly because of the doctors and also because of my ignorance about medicine and about how to interpret physical symptoms. The stress in my life also made the problem much worse. It is a long and complex story, but I have told enough to let the Christian Scientist know that my physical problems were not the result of opening myself up to "aggressive mental suggestion." I had a mild blood sugar problem, a spinal problem which caused some pinched nerves in my neck, a lot of stress, and some very inappropriate medicine that caused bizarre side effects—but we did not understand the interplay of these issues at the time. My symptoms became so complex that a doctor finally suggested I talk to a psychiatrist to determine whether the symptoms were physical or emotional in origin.

To a former Christian Scientist, going to a "shrink" was the ultimate humiliation. Christian Science teaches that our condition is the direct result of our thinking. Emotional problems represent serious spiritual inadequacy. I was not aware of anger toward anybody and felt rather emotionally normal, so I went to the consultation with a somewhat defiant attitude. I was really surprised (insulted?) when the psychiatrist suggested that I begin regular treatment.

I had no idea how to evaluate the competency of a counselor (as with medical issues, Christian Scientists are usually woefully ignorant on such matters). My psychiatrist meant well, but he used a completely inappropriate counseling technique for my type of issues (this was later confirmed by other counselors). His style of therapy took a person apart like someone takes a car engine apart and lays the pieces out on the garage floor. With an engine, each piece is cleaned and finally reassembled. This takes a long time but produces an improved engine. The problem with the style of therapy used on me was that, instead of building a better person, it reduces a person to animal instincts and manipulation. It was clear that my therapist had little use for spiritual things, because every time I talked of God working in my life he attempted to explain it away. The bad part of the therapy was that it was torturous and created some problems which took years to correct. The good part is that it broke through the denial in which I had lived all my life.

As I talked with my psychiatrist, thirty years of improperly processed emotions came pouring out. Some of the problems were minor, while others were major traumas that would have been much less damaging had they been dealt with during my childhood. The experience was a nightmare which I left after eleven months of seeing my psychiatrist four times per week. During this time I had become suicidal, even forgetting what it *meant* to want to live (this lasted for approximately one year). I went through three years of terrible anxiety and emotional pain as I dealt with my issues, first with the psychiatrist and then with a Christian counselor.

Things finally stabilized, and I had several years of relative peace as I resolved some of my issues, quit my job to concentrate on my expanding family, and got a new focus on life.

One might ask, "Where was God in all of this? Why would He allow a new, growing, dedicated Christian to go through such difficulty?" To that question I respond, "Why did He allow Joseph to go through such trauma and unfair treatment? Why did Paul have an infirmity God refused to heal? Why was Stephen martyred?"

I do not put myself or my experience on a level with those of these great Bible characters, but their trials help me to accept that God allows Christians to go through very difficult times. God always has a purpose in allowing things to happen, whether to strengthen a believer, to teach a lesson, or to accomplish some great purpose.

Whatever His purposes were in my case, one of the results was that I became more human. That sounds strange until one really studies Christian Science doctrine. I needed to undo my Christian Science thinking patterns and look at my life as I had really experienced it, instead of how I had interpreted it through my Christian Science filters. In doing so, I discovered that I was furious and resentful about a lot of things. As these skeletons emerged, I saw a side of myself that I had never recognized inside this nice person that I thought I knew. I found a depth of bitterness that really surprised me. As I came to know this dark side of myself, I began to comprehend the ugliness of sin and the gift of salvation (that Jesus gave to me as He paid for my sins on the cross). I've never learned a sweeter lesson. I also learned what it means to feel true, raw, human emotion and what it means to truly forgive. This took years of work even after the therapy was over, but the realization of my need came in the depth of my counseling experience.

God was with me throughout those years, through the Bible and through the people He put in my life. The Christian couple I mentioned earlier answered my questions, listened to my pain (much of my emotional "processing" occurred with them and not in the therapy sessions), and cared for me even though I put them through more than many friendships could tolerate. God gave me a gifted pastor who taught me much about the Bible and served as a stabilizing influence. The Lord also provided a supportive church. I learned that having given my life to my Lord, it was not mine to destroy. I look back on those difficult years as a time of valuable, faith-building growth in spite of the trauma.

Then God gave me a special gift: my husband accepted Jesus Christ as his Savior, too.

I experienced several years of relative peace as I became immersed in my expanded role of motherhood. My issues became buried under mothering, involvement in my neighborhood, church, and all of the normal activities of life. It was clear, though, that I was still troubled by my religious past. First, I had a real need to meet other people who had believed in Christian Science and later found the Jesus of the Bible. I ached for this fellowship but could not seem to progress beyond a few long distance phone conversations. I wrote to twenty-five churches in my general area asking if they knew of any former Christian Scientists who now know the Lord. Those letters led nowhere, and I felt doubly alone. My worst problem was that teaching people about Christian Science or hearing negative things about it, or its leader, would periodically trigger emotional crises.

Ten years after leaving Christian Science, I entered a crisis that produced months of ever-increasing anxiety. During this time, I read a book[2] that made me suspect that I was suffering from cult damage and not from simply missing my old religion. I became desperate to talk with someone who understood cults. A remarkable series of events led me to a residential facility for cult victims.

The Wellspring Retreat and Resource Center is located in southeastern Ohio. Nestled in the foothills of Appalachia, its privacy and nurturing atmosphere provided a wonderful setting for looking into my issues. At Wellspring, the clients live in a small alpine-style lodge which is decorated as a home. A staff member stays at the lodge to cook the meals, oversee the lodge, and "be there" for the clients between counseling sessions. The lodge is only designed to handle a few clients at a time, so the atmosphere is gentle, private, and provides a safe and homelike environment in which clients become friends and share their experiences. I had many deep, informative, and, at times, heart-wrenching conversations with the other clients who had come from a variety of cults. Through my conversations with them, I learned that much of what I was experiencing was normal for people who had lived through traumatic and abnormal circumstances.

The counselors at Wellspring are Christians, but deal with their clients on a religious level only if the clients so desire. My issues were very much tied to my religious beliefs, so we had many deep and meaningful conversations about God in the context of my therapy. I saw Christianity in action at Wellspring, both in my life and in the way the counselors and staff gave of themselves in helping the other clients. It was clear that God was working there.

One of the issues troubling me and which I needed to settle was whether Christian Science can legitimately be called a cult in the psychological sense of the word. Up to this point it had not been widely recognized as such because of the subtlety of its methods. It is difficult to imagine the mental gymnastics and suffering that go on in this group unless you have lived through them, and few of its former members really understand the amount of denial they lived under while in the group. The counselors at Wellspring are reluctant to label a group cultic unless it meets very clear criteria, so we analyzed Christian Science very carefully in terms of current secular cult theory[3] before reaching any conclusions. We finally decided that Christian Science is indeed cultic but that it functions without many of the obvious controls used by other groups (physical isolation, diet, etc.). The controls required for Christian Science are mostly mental and are inherent in its application.

Wellspring has a two-week program during which they not only provide counseling, but also run workshops educating clients about how cults function, use mind control, and trap people. Part of the education describes the dynamics of emotions and personal interactions. This information proved invaluable in helping me understand and deal with my issues.

The two-week stay at Wellspring opened up a new world to me and provided the nurturing, education, and counseling that I needed. But it was just the beginning of my healing process. After leaving Wellspring,

I wrote a paper describing Christian Science, its controls, and the emotional damage it can cause. I thought that writing the paper would provide some closure to my experience. Instead of making me feel better, it triggered a ferocious, relentless internal battle.

The root cause of my difficulties turned out to be an integration problem between the adult I am now and the child who grew up within the emotional constraints of Christian Science. Deprived of the gut-level nurturing I needed, a little childlike part of me became separated from the rest of my personality. That part remained frozen in time and aching to be nurtured. As a Christian Scientist, I never learned to meet my own deeply human needs, so that childlike part of me did not know where to turn for comfort. I unconsciously hated that part of me for all the pain it had caused over the years. To complicate the matter, that part of me was still emotionally attached to Christian Science and loyal to Mrs. Eddy. It was a little part of my identity that had been formed within the group's culture and beliefs, and giving up the Christian Science ideology felt, to "her," like a threat to my existence. All of this explains the crises I kept experiencing. Telling people about Christian Science would trigger a grieving process even though I was glad to be out of this group. Speaking against the group would trigger deep insecurities and an inner struggle which felt as though one part of me was trying to silence the other. These crises were an expression of grief, fear, and a desperate need for nurturing that I had not received as a Christian Science child.

I returned to Wellspring five weeks after writing the paper and spent several days discovering the severity of these internal conflicts. My task then became to end the conflicts by finding a way to comfort and integrate the confused, childlike part of me into the rest of my personality. I was still in a crisis, so my Wellspring counselor insisted that I find help near my home. He was able to suggest a Christian counselor who had grown up in a cult, and she and I continued the endeavor together.

Reaching the child inside was not easy. First, I had to learn to love her. My children were young like the "child" inside of me, so I began watching them and their friends very closely. I wanted to find out what their most basic needs were and how they expected these needs to be satisfied. To my utter amazement, I found that these children acted and felt just like the child inside of me.

When I made the connection between the children around me and the one inside me, I realized that the kid inside me was not an obnoxious little monster. She was simply a normal little girl who, all her life, had been crying out for her most basic human needs to be met. I developed the same compassion for this little girl that I have for any hurting child, and my resentment turned to nurturing love.

Learning to love the childlike part of me was one thing, but actually "connecting" with her proved to be much more difficult. I learned a lot about her when I attended a meeting for former Christian Scientists in 1996 (my first face-to-face contact with a group of this sort). As we shared our stories and emotional scars I realized that I was not alone. My conclusions regarding the damaging nature of this religion were not only correct, but even too conservative in many cases.

I found a wonderful, refreshing fellowship with these people. Strangely, though, I could not quite feel a part of them. I felt like an animal with my foot caught in a trap. I pulled against the chain, but could not quite reach the group. In pondering this, I realized that the childlike part of me was still fiercely loyal to Mrs. Eddy.

For the first 30 years of my life, Mrs. Eddy had been presented to me as a spiritual leader chosen by God to give His final revelation to the world. She was my leader, quoted far more often by the average Christian Scientist than were either Jesus or the Bible. There have been several biographies written which present a very dark and bizarre picture of her, but the Christian Scientists have developed their own "official" view of Mrs. Eddy which is quite worthy of respect. In short, I was stuck with a deep loyalty to this woman and no good way to evaluate her. I was sure that her writings were nonsense and was angry at what she had done to me and thousands of others, but the child inside of me remained steadfastly loyal to her.

Then a friend from the meeting sent me the memoirs of Adam Dickey,[4] Mrs. Eddy's personal secretary and one of her most loyal followers. These writings had been suppressed by the Church, but they are a gem because they show complete honesty and loyalty on Dickey's part. He describes Mrs. Eddy's strengths and also talks about some rather strange quirks. As her loyal and trusting follower, he justifies everything in terms of her status as God's messenger of truth. As I read the memoirs and watched Dickey justify her authoritarian style, quirks, and behavior in light of her teachings, a cult leader emerged from my childhood's sanitized view of her. I felt the "child" inside say "I don't want her as my leader," and the loyalty vanished. It was a tremendous sense of freedom which opened the way for further healing.

I reached another milestone when I began taking the time to really feel and listen to the childlike needs inside of me, instead of assuming that I knew what they were. This began a wonderful time of self-nurturing, and the integration process seemed to progress nicely. Then all progress stopped. It became very clear to me that I needed to return to Wellspring one more time. As I waited several weeks for the trip, a key issue began to clarify in the form of nightmares and tremendous anxiety. It turns out that the child in me was afraid to heal. She had let go of the cult leader, but her identity was still linked to the cult. For some strange reason she thought that she would cease to exist if she let go of her Christian Science view of reality. The healing process was actually becoming a threat to her life. In other words, after everything I had learned and been through in breaking free from Christian Science, the child inside me still needed "exit counseling." I had to cross this barrier before any more integration could occur. The task seemed overwhelming because of a creeping internal terror and because of the anxiety that was beginning to consume me. I couldn't attempt the task in the complexity of my life at home; I needed Wellspring's privacy and support system to get me through what I knew would be a physical and emotional ordeal.

I returned to Wellspring in February of 1997. My goal was to somehow connect with the child inside and reach her with the truth. I accomplished this over a period of three very intense days. And, eleven years after leaving Christian Science, the child let go of her old beliefs and declared her independence.

Since that time, I have been free from the hidden loyalties that bound me to Mrs. Eddy and her false concept of Christianity. I am no longer a house divided. The childlike part of me still needs special nurturing when I become involved in issues related to Christian Science, but I have discovered ways to help her instead of fighting the needs and resenting her for them. Best of all, I am free to be completely human. This is not intended to glorify man in the humanistic sense. In my frail, physical, truly human state I can yield myself to God, let Him heal my emotions, and allow Him to use me for His purposes. I can truly enjoy life with all its ups and downs, instead of having to reinterpret its stark reality through my Christian Science filters. My healing process continues as God leads me, one step at a time.

Where was God in this journey? He was everywhere. I have left a lot of details out of this story but, looking back at the total experience, I see a progression of events that are too numerous and well-timed to be coincidental. The events, their timing, and the people involved weave into a tapestry that could have been designed only by God. I am convinced that He wove this tapestry to help me understand why so many people are deeply scarred by Christian Science. I tell my story to share what I have learned. As I have told it, I have seen the light dawn in people's faces and tears come to their eyes as they finally understand why they, too, have been struggling. Helping others understand their pain opens avenues of healing to them while it adds meaning to my own experience. Best of all, it gives me a chance to glorify God. After all, He is the one who guided me to freedom.

Notes

1 Note to the Christian Scientist: In the original Greek text, words like redemption and atonement involve payment for sins and reconciliation with God. Atonement deals with restoring a broken relationship with God rather than referring to a preexisting "at-one-ment" with Him.

To trace the words to their Greek origins, see James Strong, *The Exhaustive Concordance of the Bible* (Iowa Falls, Iowa: World Bible Publishers). Strong's Concordance uses the King James Version of the *Bible.*

2   Janis Hutchinson, *Out of the Cults and Into the Church* (Grand Rapids, MI: Kregel Resources, 1994).

3   We compared Christian Science to Lifton's eight criteria for mind control, as I have done in this book.

4   Adam H. Dickey, *Memoirs of Mary Baker Eddy* (1927; reprint, Santa Clarita, CA: The Bookmark, n.d.).

Christian Science and the Bible

In Christian Science we learn that the substitution of the spiritual for the material definition of a Scriptural word often elucidates the meaning of the inspired writer. On this account [the Glossary] is added [to *Science and Health*]. It contains the metaphysical interpretation of Bible terms, giving their spiritual sense, *which is also their original meaning.* (Mary Baker Eddy, *Science and Health*, 579:1-7, emphasis added)

Sympathetic biographers have commented that Mrs. Eddy's spiritualized definitions shed "entirely new light"[1] on biblical terms and even contradict traditional Christianity.[2] Nevertheless, Christian Scientists assume, as Mrs. Eddy stated above, that her definitions do not contradict the Bible's true and original meaning. Is their assumption correct? We can begin to look at the accuracy of Christian Science by examining a few of the terms and concepts that Christians consider central to their faith.

Biblical Accuracy
Christian Science:

> [Jesus] spake of Truth and Love to artless listeners and dull disciples. His immortal words were articulated in a decaying language, and then left to the providence of God. Christian Science was to interpret them; and woman, "last at the cross," was to awaken the dull senses. . . . (Mary Baker Eddy, *Miscellaneous Writings,* 100:1-6)

Mrs. Eddy describes the disciples as dull and implies that they remained dull as they wrote the Bible. According to her statement quoted above, it took *woman*—Mary Baker Eddy and her metaphysical revelations called Christian Science—to rouse the "dull senses" long after the Bible was written. In other writings, she claims that the Bible contains "manifest mistakes in the ancient versions . . . thirty thousand different readings in the Old Testament, and . . . three hundred thousand in the New [Testament] . . ."[3] Between the dull disciples and a myriad of errors, our modern Bible must be hopelessly flawed without Mrs. Eddy and her metaphysical interpretation.

Facts about the Bible:

The Bible is the world's best-documented piece of ancient literature. At least 5,500 Greek copies have been found which reproduce all or part of the New Testament. Over fifty of these fragments are not more than 150-200 years younger than the original writings. Two major manuscripts, Codex Vaticanus (A.D. 325) and the complete text Codex Sinaiticus (A.D. 350) were copied less than 250 years after their original manuscripts. This time interval is minute compared to that of other writings whose validity is not questioned. For example, the earliest copy of Homer's *Odyssey* dates 2,200 years after the story was written.

Besides the 5,500 Greek fragments, over 18,000 ancient fragments have been found which were translated into other languages. The early Christians also quoted the New Testament text with great frequency; John Burgon catalogued over 86,000 citations made before A.D. 325. These quotations can be used to reconstruct the New Testament.[4]

Based upon the enormous number of ancient Bible manuscripts that have been discovered, it is clear that the Hebrew and Greek texts, from which our English translations were made, are an accurate representation of the original texts. These texts contain, at most, a few minor variations from the originals. There is no reason to believe that any of these variations substantially change the meaning of the Scriptures.[5]

Consider what the apostles and Jesus thought about the Bible.

According to Paul:
> All scripture is given by inspiration of God, and is profitable for doctrine, for reproof, for correction, for instruction in righteousness: That the man of God may be perfect, throughly furnished unto all good works. (2 Tim. 3:16 -17)

According to Peter:
> Knowing this first, that *no prophecy of the scripture is of any private interpretation.* For the prophecy came not in old time by the will of man: but holy men of God spake as they were moved by the Holy Ghost. (2 Pet. 1:20-21; emphasis added)

Jesus said:
> Think not that I am come to destroy the law, or the prophets: I am not come to destroy, but to fulfill. For verily I say unto you, till heaven and earth pass, one jot or one tittle shall in no wise pass from the law, till all be fulfilled. (Matt. 5:17-18; note that the "law" and the "prophets" refer to Old Testament Scriptures)

Jesus Christ

The Significance of His Name
Christian Science:

Christian Science makes a distinction between Jesus and Christ. Jesus is believed to be a mortal, material man. Christ is said to be "the divine manifestation of God."[6] In Mrs. Eddy's words:

> Christ is the ideal Truth, that comes to heal sickness and sin through Christian Science, and attributes all power to God. Jesus is the name of the man who, more than all other men, has presented Christ, the true idea of God, healing the sick and sinning and destroying the power of death. Jesus is the human man, and Christ is the divine idea; hence, the duality of Jesus the Christ. (*Science and Health*, 473:10-17)

The Bible:

The Bible treats Jesus and Christ as the same individual, using the two names interchangeably. Both the Greek term for "Christ" and the Hebrew term for "Messiah" originate from the word "anointed."[7] The term *Jesus Christ* refers to Jesus, the anointed. "Christ" and "Messiah" are equivalent and refer to a person's title rather than to a "spiritual idea."

> Paul and Timotheus, the servants of Jesus Christ, to all the saints in Christ Jesus which are at Philippi. (Phil. 1:1)

> He first findeth his own brother Simon, and saith unto him, We have found the Messias, which is, being interpreted, the Christ. (John 1:41)

> The woman saith unto him, I know that Messias cometh, which is called Christ: when he is come, he will tell us all things. (John 4:25)

His Deity
Christian Science:
Christian Science teaches that Jesus is the Son of God, but that He is not God.[8]

The Bible:
The Bible describes Jesus in many ways—as the Son of God, as a great Teacher, as the prophesied Messiah, and as a man. It also unmistakably describes Him as God (John 1:1,14). Many of the attributes given to Jesus in the Bible could only belong to God. To name a few examples, Jesus is described as eternally existent (John 1:1-2; John 17:5), the creator of all things (John 1:1,3,10; Heb. 1:2), the sustainer of all things (Heb. 1:3; Col. 1:17), and the heir of all things (Heb. 1:2). Jesus claimed the authority to forgive sins, which the scribes considered to be blasphemous as they asked the question, "Who can forgive sins but God only?" (Mark 2:3-10). Jesus spoke of having the authority both to lay down His life and to take it up again (John 10:17-18). He used the term "I AM" in reference to Himself (John 8:58), equating Himself with the God of the Old Testament. He did not rebuke Thomas for calling Him God (John 20:28). Also note that God killed Herod for accepting this title (Acts 12:21-23). Jesus accepted worship (John 9:35-38; Luke 24:51-52), in stark contrast to both the angels (Rev 22: 8-9) and His disciples (Acts 10:25-26; Acts 14:8-15). Devout Jews prayed only to God, but Stephen prayed to Jesus as he was being stoned to death (Acts 7:59). Paul also made a reference to the deity of Jesus when he instructed the elders from Ephesus to "feed the church of God, which he hath purchased with his own blood" (Acts 20:28).

> In the beginning was the Word, and the Word was with God, and the Word was God. . . . And the Word was made flesh, and dwelt among us, (and we beheld his glory, the glory as of the only begotten of the Father,) full of grace and truth. (John 1:1,14)

In the beginning was the Word, and the Word was with God, and the Word was God. The same was in the beginning with God. (John 1:1-2)

And now, O Father, glorify thou me with thine own self with the glory which I had with thee before the world was. (John 17:5)

In the beginning was the Word, and the Word was with God, and the Word was God. . . . All things were made by him; and without him was not any thing made that was made. . . . He was in the world, and the world was made by him, and the world knew him not. (John 1:1, 3, 10)

[God] Hath in these last days spoken unto us by his Son, whom he hath appointed heir of all things, by whom also he made the worlds. (Heb. 1:2)

Who being the brightness of his glory, and the express image of his person, and upholding all things by the word of his power, when he had by himself purged our sins, sat down on the right hand of the Majesty on high. (Heb. 1:3)

Translation from New International Version:

The Son is the radiance of God's glory and the exact representation of his being, sustaining all things by his powerful word. After he had provided purification for sins, he sat down at the right hand of the Majesty in heaven. (Heb. 1:3)

And he is before all things, and by him all things consist. (Col. 1:17)

Hath in these last days spoken unto us by his Son, whom he hath appointed heir of all things, by whom also he made the worlds. (Heb. 1:2)

And they come unto him, bringing one sick of the palsy, which was borne of four. And when they could not come nigh unto him for the press, they uncovered the roof where he was: and when they had broken it up, they let down the bed wherein the sick of the palsy lay. When Jesus saw their faith, he said unto the sick of the palsy, Son, thy sins be forgiven thee. But there were certain of the scribes sitting there, and reasoning in their hearts, Why doth this man thus speak blasphemies? who can forgive sins but God only? And immediately when Jesus perceived in his spirit that they so reasoned within themselves, he said unto them, Why reason ye these things in your hearts? Whether is it easier to say to the sick of the palsy, Thy sins be forgiven thee; or to say, Arise, and take up thy bed, and walk? But that ye may know that the Son of man hath power on earth to forgive sins. (Mark 2:3-10)

Therefore doth my Father love me, because I lay down my life, that I might take it again. No man taketh it from me, but I lay it down of myself. I have power to lay it down, and I have power to take it again. This commandment have I received of my Father. (John 10:17-18)

Jesus said unto them, Verily, verily, I say unto you, Before Abraham was, I am. (John 8:58)

And Thomas answered and said unto him, My Lord and my God. (John 20:28)

And upon a set day Herod, arrayed in royal apparel, sat upon his throne, and made an oration unto them. And the people gave a shout, saying, It is the voice of a god, and not of a man. And immediately the angel of the Lord smote him, because he gave not God the glory: and he was eaten of worms, and gave up the ghost. (Acts 12:21-23)

Jesus heard that they had cast him out; and when he had found him, he said unto him, Dost thou believe on the Son of God? He answered and said, Who is he, Lord, that I might believe on him? And Jesus said unto him, Thou hast both seen him, and it is he that talketh with thee. And he said, Lord, I believe. And he worshipped him. (John 9:35- 38)

And it came to pass, while he blessed them, he was parted from them, and carried up into heaven. And they worshipped him, and returned to Jerusalem with great joy. (Luke 24:51-52)

And I John saw these things, and heard them. And when I had heard and seen, I fell down to worship before the feet of the angel which showed me these things. Then saith he unto me, See thou do it not: for I am thy fellowservant, and of thy brethren the prophets, and of them which keep the sayings of this book: worship God. (Rev. 22:8-9)

And as Peter was coming in, Cornelius met him, and fell down at his feet, and worshipped him. But Peter took him up, saying, Stand up; I myself also am a man. (Acts 10:25-26)

And there sat a certain man at Lystra, impotent in his feet, being a cripple from his mother's womb, who never had walked: The same heard Paul speak: who steadfastly beholding him, and perceiving that he had faith to be healed, Said with a loud voice, Stand upright on thy feet. And he leaped and walked. And when the people saw what Paul had done, they lifted up their voices, saying in the speech of Lycaonia, The gods are come down to us in the likeness of men. And they called Barnabas, Jupiter; and Paul, Mercurius, because he was the chief speaker. Then the priest of Jupiter, which was before their city, brought oxen and garlands unto the gates, and would have done sacrifice with the people.

Which when the apostles, Barnabas and Paul, heard of, they rent their clothes, and ran in among the people, crying out, And saying, Sirs, why do ye these things? We also are men of like passions with you, and preach unto you that ye should turn from these vanities unto the living God, which made heaven, and earth, and the sea, and all things that are therein. (Acts 14:8-15)

And they stoned Stephen, calling upon God, and saying, Lord Jesus, receive my spirit. (Acts 7:59)

Take heed therefore unto yourselves, and to all the flock, over the which the Holy Ghost hath made you overseers, to feed the church of God, which he hath purchased with his own blood. (Acts 20:28)

The Purpose of His Crucifixion
Christian Science:

Christian Science teaches that the true, spiritual man is unfallen and sinless. The sinning, mortal man we see is said to be an illusion which can be overcome by understanding and demonstrating man's true relationship to God.

According to Mrs. Eddy, Jesus' mission was to demonstrate the reality of man's spiritual nature and to prove man's dominion over the beliefs of sin, sickness, and death. His crucifixion "saved" man from sin, disease, and death by demonstrating their unreality and showing man's dominion over them. Along with this teaching, Christian Science maintains that Jesus did not really die and that His bodily sacrifice and shed blood were not, in themselves, sufficient payment for the sins of mankind.

His disciples believed Jesus to be dead while he was hidden in the sepulcher, whereas he was alive, demonstrating within the narrow tomb the power of Spirit to overrule mortal, material sense. . . . Our Master fully and finally demonstrated divine Science in his victory over death and the grave. (*Science and Health,* 44:28-31, 45:6-7)

Does erudite theology regard the crucifixion of Jesus chiefly as providing a ready pardon for all sinners who ask for it and are willing to be forgiven? . . . Then we must differ. . . .

The efficacy of the crucifixion lay in the practical affection and goodness it demonstrated for mankind. The truth had been lived among men; but until they saw that it enabled their Master to triumph over the grave, his own disciples could not admit such an event to be possible. . . . The spiritual essence of blood is sacrifice. The efficacy of Jesus' spiritual offering is infinitely greater than can be expressed by our sense of human blood. The material blood of Jesus was no more efficacious to cleanse from sin when it was shed upon "the accursed tree," than when it was flowing in his veins as he went daily about his Father's business. (*Science and Health,* 24:20-31, 25:3-9)

One sacrifice, however great, is insufficient to pay the debt of sin. The atonement requires constant self-immolation on the sinner's part. That God's wrath should be vented upon His beloved Son, is divinely unnatural. Such a theory is man-made. (*Science and Health,* 23:3-7)

The Bible:

The Bible clearly disagrees with Christian Science regarding the purpose of Jesus' crucifixion. It describes God as a loving God, but also makes it clear that His holiness and divine justice demand that sin must be judged and punished. The Bible states that, because of Jesus' sinless nature, he was qualified to bear the judgment that sinful mankind deserves. His death was, therefore, substitutionary. By His death He became the Savior of the lost (2 Cor. 5:21, Heb. 10:5-14, 1 Pet. 3:18).

For he hath made him to be sin for us, who knew no sin; that we might be made the righteousness of God in him. (2 Cor. 5:21)

According to the translation from New International Version, when Christ came into the world, He said:

Sacrifice and offering you did not desire, but a body you prepared for me; with burnt offerings and sin offerings you were not pleased. Then I said, "Here I am—it is written about me in the scroll—I have come to do your will, O God." First he said, "Sacrifices and offerings, burnt offerings and sin offerings you did not desire, nor were you pleased with them" (although the law required them to be made). Then he said, "Here I am, I have come to do your will." He sets aside the first to establish the second. And by that will, we have been made holy through the sacrifice of the body of Jesus Christ once for all. Day after day every priest stands and performs his religious duties; again and again he offers the same sacrifices, which can never take away sins. But when this priest had offered for all time one sacrifice for sins, he sat down at the right hand of God. Since that time he waits for his enemies to be made his footstool, because by one sacrifice he has made perfect forever those who are being made holy. (Heb. 10:5-14)

For Christ also hath once suffered for sins, the just for the unjust, that he might bring us to God, being put to death in the flesh, but quickened by the Spirit. (1 Pet. 3:18)

The importance of Jesus' sacrificial death and the shedding of His blood are also supported by the verses listed below. These verses relate Jesus' crucifixion to the form of animal sacrifice performed under Jewish law, and make sense of the Bible's reference to Him as the "Lamb of God": John 1:29; Heb. 10:10; Rom. 4:25; 2 Cor. 5:21; Rom. 5:18-19; John 3:16; Heb. 9:15; Gal. 1:3-4; 1 Pet. 1:18-19; Rom. 3:23-25; Eph. 1:7; Heb. 9:22-28.

The next day John seeth Jesus coming unto him, and saith, Behold the Lamb of God, which taketh away the sin of the world. (John 1:29)

By the which will we are sanctified through the offering of the body of Jesus Christ once for all. (Heb. 10:10)

Who was delivered for our offences, and was raised again for our justification. (Rom. 4:25)

For he hath made him to be sin for us, who knew no sin; that we might be made the righteousness of God in him. (2 Cor. 5:21)

Therefore as by the offence of one judgment came upon all men to condemnation; even so by the righteousness of one the free gift came upon all men unto justification of life. For as by one man's disobedience many were made sinners, so by the obedience of one shall many be made righteous. (Rom. 5:18-19)

For God so loved the world, that he gave his only begotten Son, that whosoever believeth in him should not perish, but have everlasting life. (John 3:16)

And for this cause he is the mediator of the new testament, that by means of death, for the redemption of the transgressions that were under the first testament, they which are called might receive the promise of eternal inheritance. (Heb. 9:15)

Grace be to you and peace from God the Father, and from our Lord Jesus Christ, Who gave himself for our sins, that he might deliver us from this present evil world, according to the will of God and our Father. (Gal. 1:3-4)

Forasmuch as ye know that ye were not redeemed with corruptible things, as silver and gold, from your vain conversation received by tradition from your fathers; But with the precious blood of Christ, as of a lamb without blemish and without spot. (1 Pet. 1:18-19)

For all have sinned, and come short of the glory of God; Being justified freely by his grace through the redemption that is in Christ Jesus: Whom God hath set forth to be a propitiation through faith in his blood, to declare his righteousness for the remission of sins that are past, through the forbearance of God. (Rom. 3:23-25)

In whom we have redemption through his blood, the forgiveness of sins, according to the riches of his grace. (Eph. 1:7)

And almost all things are by the law purged with blood; and without shedding of blood is no remission. It was therefore necessary that the patterns of things in the heavens should be purified with these; but the heavenly things themselves with better sacrifices than these. For Christ is not entered into the holy places made with hands, which are the figures of the true; but into heaven itself, now to appear in the presence of God for us: Nor yet that he should offer himself often, as the high priest entereth into the holy place every year with blood of others; For then must he often have suffered since the foundation of the world: but now once in the end of the world hath he appeared to put away sin by the sacrifice of himself. And as it is appointed unto men once to die, but after this the judgment: So Christ was once offered to bear the sins of many; and unto them that look for him shall he appear the second time without sin unto salvation. (Heb. 9:22-28)

The Bible says that Jesus physically died and that He arose from the dead in His original body, although it was now glorified (John 20:20; 1 Cor. 15:3-6).

> And when he had so said, he showed unto them his hands and his side. Then were the disciples glad, when they saw the Lord. (John 20:20)

> For I delivered unto you first of all that which I also received, how that Christ died for our sins according to the scriptures; And that he was buried, and that he rose again the third day according to the scriptures: And that he was seen of Cephas, then of the twelve: After that, he was seen of above five hundred brethren at once; of whom the greater part remain unto this present, but some are fallen asleep. (1 Cor. 15:3-6)

In ascending, He became the Head over the church of believers. In this ministry He intercedes and advocates for the saved (Eph. 1:22-23: Heb. 7:25, 1 John 2:1). The term "saved" refers to those who have accepted Jesus as their Savior and will spend eternity with Him (1 Thess. 4:15-17).

> And hath put all things under his feet, and gave him to be the head over all things to the church, Which is his body, the fullness of him that filleth all in all. (Eph. 1:22-23)

> Wherefore he is able also to save them to the uttermost that come unto God by him, seeing he ever liveth to make intercession for them. (Heb. 7:25)

> My little children, these things write I unto you, that ye sin not. And if any man sin, we have an advocate with the Father, Jesus Christ the righteous. (1 John 2:1)

For this we say unto you by the word of the Lord, that we which are alive and remain unto the coming of the Lord shall not prevent them which are asleep. For the Lord himself shall descend from heaven with a shout, with the voice of the archangel, and with the trump of God: and the dead in Christ shall rise first: Then we which are alive and remain shall be caught up together with them in the clouds, to meet the Lord in the air: and so shall we ever be with the Lord. (1 Thess. 4:15-17)

The Holy Spirit

Christian Science:

Mrs. Eddy claims that the Holy Spirit is Christian Science. To understand this from the quotations listed below, the reader must realize that Mrs. Eddy uses the terms "Divine Science" and "Christian Science" interchangeably (*Science and Health*, 127:9-12), and that the Bible uses the names Holy Ghost, Holy Spirit, and Comforter interchangeably. Mrs. Eddy states:

In the words of St. John: "He shall give you another Comforter, that he may abide with you *forever*." This Comforter I understand to be Divine Science. (*Science and Health*, 55:27-29)

[Jesus'] students then received the Holy Ghost. By this is meant, that by all they had witnessed and suffered, they were roused to an enlarged understanding of divine Science, even to the spiritual interpretation and discernment of Jesus' teachings and demonstrations, which gave them a faint conception of the Life which is God. . . . The influx of light was sudden. It was sometimes an overwhelming power as on the Day of Pentecost. (*Science and Health*, 46:30-47:3, 47:7-9)

The Bible:

The Bible identifies the Holy Spirit not as Christian Science, but as God and as part of the Trinity. He is a personality rather than a set of qualities. He listens to people (Acts 5:3-4), helps us to pray (Rom. 8:26-27), can be grieved (Eph. 4:30), instructs believers (Acts 10:19-20; Acts 13:2; 1 Tim. 4:1), rebukes the world (John 16:7-8), comforts believers (John 14:16-17), indwells believers (Rom. 8:9; 1 Cor. 6:19-20; 1 Cor. 3:16), and seals (or earmarks) believers for the day of redemption (Eph. 1:13-14; Eph. 4:30).

> But Peter said, Ananias, why hath Satan filled thine heart to lie to the Holy Ghost, and to keep back part of the price of the land? Whiles it remained, was it not thine own? And after it was sold, was it not in thine own power? why hast thou conceived this thing in thine heart? thou hast not lied unto men, but unto God. (Acts 5:3-4)

> Likewise the Spirit also helpeth our infirmities: for we know not what we should pray for as we ought: but the Spirit itself maketh intercession for us with groanings which cannot be uttered. And he that searcheth the hearts knoweth what is the mind of the Spirit, because he maketh intercession for the saints according to the will of God. (Rom. 8:26-27)

> And grieve not the holy Spirit of God, whereby ye are sealed unto the day of redemption. (Eph. 4:30)

> While Peter thought on the vision, the Spirit said unto him, Behold, three men seek thee. Arise therefore, and get thee down, and go with them, doubting nothing: for I have sent them. (Acts 10:19-20)

As they ministered to the Lord, and fasted, the Holy Ghost said, Separate me Barnabas and Saul for the work whereunto I have called them. (Acts 13:2)

Now the Spirit speaketh expressly, that in the latter times some shall depart from the faith, giving heed to seducing spirits, and doctrines of devils. (1 Tim. 4:1)

Nevertheless I tell you the truth; It is expedient for you that I go away: for if I go not away, the Comforter will not come unto you; but if I depart, I will send him unto you. And when he is come, he will reprove the world of sin, and of righteousness, and of judgment. (John 16:7-8)

And I will pray the Father, and he shall give you another Comforter, that he may abide with you for ever; Even the Spirit of truth; whom the world cannot receive, because it seeth him not, neither knoweth him: but ye know him; for he dwelleth with you, and shall be in you. (John 14:16-17)

But ye are not in the flesh, but in the Spirit, if so be that the Spirit of God dwell in you. Now if any man have not the Spirit of Christ, he is none of his. (Rom. 8:9)

What? know ye not that your body is the temple of the Holy Ghost which is in you, which ye have of God, and ye are not your own? For ye are bought with a price: therefore glorify God in your body, and in your spirit, which are God's. (1 Cor. 6:19- 20)

Know ye not that ye are the temple of God, and that the Spirit of God dwelleth in you? (1 Cor. 3:16)

In whom ye also trusted, after that ye heard the word of truth, the gospel of your salvation: in whom also after that ye believed, ye were sealed with that holy Spirit of promise, Which is the earnest of our inheritance until the redemption of the purchased possession, unto the praise of his glory. (Eph. 1:13-14)

And grieve not the holy Spirit of God, whereby ye are sealed unto the day of redemption. (Eph. 4:30)

These verses show the Holy Spirit influencing people (as by teaching) and being influenced by people (as by being grieved). He is referred to by the pronoun "He" and is someone with whom people can communicate (as when Ananias lied to Him in Acts 5:3). These characteristics describe a personality. They do not describe "the law of God, the law of good" or a "scientific system of diving healing," definitions that Mrs. Eddy gives for Christian Science.[9]

The Trinity

Although the term "Trinity" is not in the Bible, both traditional Christianity and Christian Science have incorporated the word in their doctrines. While Christianity is referring to the Father, the Son, and the Holy Spirit as it defines them, Christian Science uses the word trinity to describe a tri-unity of Life, Truth, and Love.

Christian Science:

Life, Truth, and Love constitute the triune Person called God,— that is, the triply divine Principle, Love. They represent a trinity in unity, three in one,—the same in essence, though multiform in office: God the Father-Mother; Christ the spiritual idea of sonship; divine Science [i.e., Christian Science] or the Holy Comforter. These three express in divine Science the threefold, essential nature of the infinite. They also indicate the divine Principle of scientific being, the intelligent relation of God to man and the universe. (*Science and Health*, 331:26-332:3)

The name Elohim [a Hebrew term for God] is in the plural, but this plurality of Spirit does not imply more than one God, nor does it imply three persons in one. It relates to the oneness, the tri-unity of Life, Truth, and Love. (*Science and Health*, 515:17-20)

The theory of three persons in one God (that is, a personal Trinity or Tri-unity) suggests polytheism rather than the one ever-present I AM. (*Science and Health*, 256:9-11)

The Bible:
Traditional Christianity teaches that there is one God but that there are three persons in the godhead (the godhead refers to the nature or essence of God). This concept is baffling to the human mind but is substantiated by the Bible. The Father is called God in Romans 1:7, the Son is called God in Hebrews 1:8 (also see section on Jesus' deity), and the Holy Spirit is called God in Acts 5:3-4. We accept the concept of the Trinity by faith, for the Bible says that He does not intend for us to understand absolutely everything about Him (Rom. 11:33-34).

To all that be in Rome, beloved of God, called to be saints: Grace to you and peace from God our Father, and the Lord Jesus Christ. (Rom. 1:7)

But unto the Son he saith, Thy throne, O God, is for ever and ever: a sceptre of righteousness is the sceptre of thy kingdom. (Heb. 1:8)

But Peter said, Ananias, why hath Satan filled thine heart to lie to the Holy Ghost, and to keep back part of the price of the land? Whiles it remained, was it not thine own? and after it

was sold, was it not in thine own power? why hast thou conceived this thing in thine heart? thou hast not lied unto men,
but unto God. (Acts 5:3-4)

O the depth of the riches both of the wisdom and knowledge
of God! how unsearchable are his judgments, and his ways
past finding out! For who hath known the mind of the Lord?
or who hath been his counselor? (Rom. 11:33-34)

The members of the Trinity are not limited to finite, material bodies,
but they are indeed persons. Each of them has personality characteristics
such as emotion and will. They are three Persons, but one God. The Bible
lists them together, without ranking (Matt. 28:18-19; 2 Cor. 13:14).

And Jesus came and spake unto them, saying, All power is giv-
en unto me in heaven and in earth. Go ye therefore, and teach
all nations, baptizing them in the name of the Father, and of
the Son, and of the Holy Ghost. (Matt. 28:18-19)

The grace of the Lord Jesus Christ, and the love of God, and
the communion of the Holy Ghost, be with you all. Amen. (2
Cor. 13:14)

Heaven and Hell

Christian Science:
Christian Science teaches that heaven and hell are states of consciousness rather than actual locations.

HEAVEN. Harmony; the reign of Spirit; government by divine
Principle; spirituality; bliss; the atmosphere of Soul. (*Science
and Health*, 587:25-27)

HELL. Mortal belief; error; lust; remorse; hatred; revenge; sin; sickness; death; suffering and self-destruction; self-imposed agony; effects of sin; that which "worketh abomination or maketh a lie." (*Science and Health,* 588:1-4)

The sinner makes his own hell by doing evil, and the saint his own heaven by doing right. (*Science and Health,* 266:20-21)

To reach heaven, the harmony of being, we must understand the divine Principle of being. (*Science and Health,* 6:14-16)

The evil beliefs which originate in mortals are hell. (*Science and Health,* 266:26-27)

The Bible:
The Bible describes heaven and hell as actual places. Heaven is the place where God resides; true followers of Jesus Christ will spend eternity with Him in heaven. Hell is the place God created for Satan and his fallen angels to be punished for their rebellion against Him; people who are not followers of Jesus Christ will spend eternity in hell (Mark 16:19; Luke 10:20; Matt. 18:10-11; John 14:2-4, 6; 2 Thess. 1:7; Matt. 16:17-18; Matt. 25:41, 46; Mark 9:43-44; 2 Pet. 2:4, 9; Rev. 20:10, 15).

So then after the Lord had spoken unto them, he was received up into heaven, and sat on the right hand of God. (Mark 16:19)

Notwithstanding in this rejoice not, that the spirits are subject unto you; but rather rejoice, because your names are written in heaven. (Luke 10:20)

Take heed that ye despise not one of these little ones; for I say unto you, That in heaven their angels do always behold the face of my Father which is in heaven. For the Son of man is come to save that which was lost. (Matt. 18:10-11)

In my Father's house are many mansions: if it were not so, I would have told you. I go to prepare a place for you. And if I go and prepare a place for you, I will come again, and receive you unto myself; that where I am, there ye may be also. And whither I go ye know, and the way ye know. . . . Jesus saith unto him, I am the way, the truth, and the life: no man cometh unto the Father, but by me. (John 14:2-4, 6)

And to you who are troubled rest with us, when the Lord Jesus shall be revealed from heaven with his mighty angels. (2 Thess. 1:7)

And Jesus answered and said unto him, Blessed art thou, Simon Barjona: for flesh and blood hath not revealed it unto thee, but my Father which is in heaven. And I say also unto thee, That thou art Peter, and upon this rock I will build my church; and the gates of hell shall not prevail against it. (Matt. 16:17-18)

Then shall he say also unto them on the left hand, Depart from me, ye cursed, into everlasting fire, prepared for the devil and his angels: . . . And these shall go away into everlasting punishment: but the righteous into life eternal. (Matt. 25:41, 46)

And if thy hand offend thee, cut it off: it is better for thee to enter into life maimed, than having two hands to go into hell, into the fire that never shall be quenched: Where their worm dieth not, and the fire is not quenched. (Mark 9:43-44)

For if God spared not the angels that sinned, but cast them down to hell, and delivered them into chains of darkness, to be reserved unto judgment; . . . The Lord knoweth how to deliver the godly out of temptations, and to reserve the unjust unto the day of judgement to be punished. (2 Pet. 2:4, 9)

And the devil that deceived them was cast into the lake of fire and brimstone, where the beast and the false prophet are, and shall be tormented day and night for ever and ever. . . . And whosoever was not found written in the book of life was cast into the lake of fire. (Rev. 20:10, 15)

Judgment

Christian Science:
Christian Science teaches that there is no final "judgment day." Each person obtains salvation (from his or her belief in materiality) through a process of spiritual growth that begins in this life and continues after death. The death experience does not play a part in the growth process.

No final judgment awaits mortals, for the judgment-day of wisdom comes hourly and continually, even the judgment by which mortal man is divested of all material error. (*Science and Health,* 291:28-31)

As man falleth asleep, so shall he awake. As death findeth mortal man, so shall he be after death, until probation and growth shall effect the needed change. (*Science and Health,* 291:22-25)

When the last mortal fault is destroyed, then the final trump will sound which will end the battle of Truth with error and mortality. (*Science and Health,* 292:1-3)

The Bible:
The Bible states that each person will be judged by God. That judgment will be a one time event rather than a progressive process (Matt. 7:21-23; John 5:28-29; Heb. 9:27-28; Rom. 2:16; Rom. 2:5-6).

> Not every one that saith unto me, Lord, Lord, shall enter into the kingdom of heaven; but he that doeth the will of my Father which is in heaven. Many will say to me in that day, Lord, Lord, have we not prophesied in thy name? and in thy name have cast out devils? and in thy name done many wonderful works? And then will I profess unto them, I never knew you: depart from me, ye that work iniquity. (Matt. 7:21-23)

> Marvel not at this: for the hour is coming, in the which all that are in the graves shall hear his voice, And shall come forth; they that have done good, unto the resurrection of life; and they that have done evil, unto the resurrection of damnation. (John 5:28-29)

> And as it is appointed unto men once to die, but after this the judgment: So Christ was once offered to bear the sins of many; and unto them that look for him shall he appear the second time without sin unto salvation. (Heb. 9:27-28)

> In the day when God shall judge the secrets of men by Jesus Christ according to my gospel. (Rom. 2:16)

> But after thy hardness and impenitent heart treasurest up unto thyself wrath against the day of wrath and revelation of the righteous judgment of God; Who will render to every man according to his deeds. (Rom. 2:5-6)

Salvation

Christian Science:

Christian Science teaches that salvation is a progressive process that saves a person not from hell, but from his or her belief in materiality.

> SALVATION: Life, Truth, and Love understood and demonstrated as supreme over all; sin, sickness and death destroyed. (*Science and Health*, 593:20-22)

> (Also see references in Judgment section.)

The Bible:

People cannot enter heaven unless they admit that they have sinned and accept, by faith, the sacrifice Jesus made by dying for their sins on the cross. Salvation cannot be attained by church membership, good works, or any means other than accepting Jesus' sacrifice. Good works are an important part of the believer's life and an outward expression of his faith, but they, in themselves, do not earn him salvation (John 3:5-7; Rom. 5:8-9; Eph. 2:8-9; 1 Pet. 1:18-19,23; John 1:12; Rom. 1:16; Gal. 3:24).

> Jesus answered, Verily, verily, I say unto thee, Except a man be born of water and of the Spirit, he cannot enter into the kingdom of God. That which is born of the flesh is flesh; and that which is born of the Spirit is spirit. Marvel not that I said unto thee, Ye must be born again. (John 3:5-7)

> But God commendeth his love toward us, in that, while we were yet sinners, Christ died for us. Much more then, being now justified by his blood, we shall be saved from wrath through him. (Rom. 5:8-9)

For by grace are ye saved through faith; and that not of yourselves: it is the gift of God: Not of works, lest any man should
boast. (Eph. 2:8-9)

Forasmuch as ye know that ye were not redeemed with corruptible things, as silver and gold, from your vain conversation received by tradition from your fathers; But with the
precious blood of Christ, as of a lamb without blemish and
without spot: . . . Being born again, not of corruptible seed, but
of incorruptible, by the word of God, which liveth and abideth
for ever. (1 Pet. 1:18-19, 23)

But as many as received him, to them gave he power to become the sons of God, even to them that believe on his name.
(John 1:12)

For I am not ashamed of the gospel of Christ: for it is the power of God unto salvation to every one that believeth; to the
Jew first, and also to the Greek. (Rom. 1:16)

Wherefore the law was our schoolmaster to bring us unto
Christ, that we might be justified by faith. (Gal. 3:24)

The Bottom Line: Illumination or Contradiction?

Mrs. Eddy teaches that the Bible is tainted by mistakes and uninspired
verses. Historical records, the apostles, and Jesus claim that the Bible is
reliable. Mrs. Eddy teaches that Jesus died (to human belief) to prove
that death is unreal. The Bible says that Jesus died physically and that
he died to take the punishment for our sins. Mrs. Eddy teaches that the
Holy Spirit is Christian Science. The Bible teaches that the Holy Spirit
is part of the godhead. Mrs. Eddy teaches that heaven and hell are not
real. The Bible says that they are very real places. Mrs. Eddy teaches that
salvation is our own responsibility, dependent on our understanding and

demonstrating "Life, Truth, and Love" as defined by Christian Science. The Bible teaches that salvation is a free gift, paid for by the blood of Jesus Christ.

Are Mrs. Eddy's statements illuminating the Bible or contradicting it?

Christianity is Not Complicated

I sometimes hear from people who reject Christianity and, indeed, any organized religion. They sense an attitude of intolerance among Christians ("believe what we believe or you will go to hell"). They point to corruption among some of the prominent Christian leaders and to atrocities carried out in the name of religion. They resent the arbitrary rules imposed by some churches in the name of spiritual purity. I understand their concerns.

Much harm has been done in the name of Christianity. Christianity becomes tainted when a leader claims to have a unique connection to God and uses this "special revelation" to interpret the Bible's message and standards. Christianity seems shallow and even crazy when people over-emphasize God's love and rely too much on feelings and emotional experiences. The religion seems cruel when God's judgment is overemphasized to the exclusion of His love. It becomes a frightening burden when good works are emphasized as the means of winning salvation. But none of these perversions represent the Christianity taught in the Bible.

Biblical Christianity becomes clear when the Bible is taken as a whole. I see the following scenario: God is a God of love *and* of justice. He loves us deeply but cannot tolerate acts and attitudes that violate His perfect standards. Because God wants us to love Him freely, he gives us the option to either follow or reject Him. God knows that, even if we do love Him, we cannot live up to His perfect standards of morality, honesty, and the like. Instead of dooming us because of His unattainable standards, He provided a way out. He sent his Son Jesus to live among us and then to take the punishment for our sins. He is examining our attitude here—are we willing to admit our need for help, accept the gift that Jesus gave us, and let Him set our standards and be our guide? In other words, are we willing to let God be God? Or do we want to do things our own way, either striving to achieve His perfect standards through our own efforts or ignoring Him and setting our own standards?

The root issue is our attitude toward God and His supremacy. According to the Bible, Satan's root sin was his attitude—he wanted to be like God (Isa. 14:13-14) and to have both the angels and Jesus follow him instead of God (2 Pet. 2:4, Matt. 4:8-10). In the same manner, Eve's sin was an attitude problem. She ate the fruit in disobedience because she wanted to know both good and evil, just like God (Gen. 3:5). God does not tolerate insubordination for long. He threw Satan and the rebellious angels out of heaven, and it appears that he does not want rebellious people in heaven either.

As I see it, Christianity is simple. Admit that you sin and that you cannot help but sin. Tell God that you don't want your sinful nature to interfere with your relationship with Him, and then accept the provision He made—Jesus' sacrificial death. Tell Him that you want Him to be your leader and your guide through life; in other words, give him the honor He is due as your Creator. Then read the Bible and follow its principles. Look at the lives of the Bible characters and see how they handled the trials of daily life. Watch how they confessed their sins and maintained an ongoing relationship with God through prayer. Learn how to treat other people by studying Jesus' teachings and the Epistles.

The Bible is our guide to Christian living. It is not antiquated or full of mistakes. Its words declare just what God wanted us to hear; they do not need to be spiritually interpreted. The Bible is very clear about issues such as morality, integrity, and God's supremacy. In those areas it is important to adhere to God's standards, even if that adherence is not understood by those who do not follow the Bible. In other areas the Bible gives general principles but leaves room for individual interpretation.

God wants us to function as a body of believers—to maintain some form of organized religion. He told us not to stop meeting together (Heb. 10:25), and He also explained that a group of believers functions as a unit in order to help one another (e.g., 1 Cor. 12). It is important to join a group of believers that looks to the Bible (not its leader) as its source of guidance, that balances God's love and justice, and which takes the Bible's absolute standards literally while giving its members freedom of conscience in areas not specified in the Bible.

When practiced as taught by the Bible, Christianity is a blessing rather than a burden or a verbal weapon. It provides the security of forgiveness, the joy of communing with God, and the freedom to be human in spite of our imperfections.

Notes

1   Richard A. Nenneman, *Persistent Pilgrim: The Life of Mary Baker Eddy* (Etna, NH: Nebbadoon Press, 1997), 190-192.

2   Yvonne Caché von Fettweis and Robert Townsend Warneck, *Mary Baker Eddy: Christian Healer,* (Boston: The Christian Science Publishing Society, 1998), 113.

3   Mary Baker Eddy, *Science and Health with Key to the Scriptures* (Boston: Published under the Will of Mary Baker G. Eddy, 1934), 139:16-19.

4   Josh McDowell and Don Stewart, *Answers to Tough Questions Skeptics Ask about the Christian Faith* (Wheaton, IL: Tyndale House Publishers, Inc., 1980), 21-23. Also see Josh McDowell, *Evidence that Demands a Verdict,* vol. 1 (San Bernardino, CA: Here's Life Publishers, Inc., 1972, 1979), chapter 4.

5   Josh McDowell, *Evidence that Demands a Verdict,* vol. 1 (San Bernardino, CA: Here's Life Publishers, Inc., 1972, 1979), chapter 4.

6   Mary Baker Eddy, *Science and Health,* 583:10.

7   To explore the Greek and Hebrew origins of biblical terms, see James Strong, *The Exhaustive Concordance of the Bible* (Iowa Falls, IA: World Bible Publishers).

8   Mary Baker Eddy, *Science and Health,* 361:10-13.

9   Mary Baker Eddy, *Rudimental Divine Science* (Boston: Published by the Trustees under the Will of Mary Baker G. Eddy, 1936), 1:2; *Science and Health,* 123:16-18.

Resources

Books
See Chapter Three for a list of books used as reference material for *Perfect Peril*. The list includes books both supporting and not supporting Christian Science.

History of Christian Science
Fraser, Caroline. God's Perfect Child: Living and Dying in the Christian Science Church. New York: Metropolitan Books, 1999.

Gill, Gillian. Mary Baker Eddy. Cambridge: Perseus Books, 1998.

Memoirs by Former Christian Scientists
Simmons, Thomas. The Unseen Shore: Memories of a Christian Science Childhood. Boston: Beacon, 1991.

Wilson, Barbara. Blue Windows: A Christian Science Childhood. New York: Picador USA, 1997.

Cults and Mind Control – General Information
Cialdini, Robert B. *Influence: Science and Practice, second edition,* Arizona State University: Harper-Collins Publishers, 1988, 1985.

Hassan, Steven. *Combating Cult Mind Control.* Rochester, VT: Park Street Press, 1988, 1990.

Hassan, Steven. *Releasing the Bonds: Empowering People to Think for Themselves.* Somerville, MA: Freedom of Mind Press, 2000.

Lifton, Robert Jay. *Thought Reform and the Psychology of Totalism: A Study of "Brainwashing" in China.* 1961, reprint; Chapel Hill: The University of North Carolina Press, 1989, chapter 22.

Singer, Margaret Thaler with Lalich, Janja. *Cults in Our Midst: The Hidden Menace in Our Everyday Lives.* San Francisco: Jossey-Bass Publishers, 1995.

Cults – Books from a Christian Perspective

Hutchinson, Janis. Out of the Cults and Into the Church: Understanding & Encouraging Ex-Cultists. Grand Rapids, MI: Kregel Resources, 1994.

Martin, Walter. The Kingdom of the Cults. Minneapolis, MN: Bethany House Publishers, 1997.

Scott, Latayne C. Why We Left A Cult: Six People Tell Their Stories. Grand Rapids, MI: Baker Book House, 1993. (Two of the people interviewed are former Christian Scientists)

Christianity

McDowell, Josh & Larson, Bart. *Jesus: A Biblical Defense of His Deity.* San Bernardino: Here's Life Publishers, Inc., 1983.

McDowell, Josh. *Evidence that Demands a Verdict: Historical Evidences for the Christian Faith,* 2 vols. Here's Life Publishers, Inc., 1972, 1979.

McDowell, Josh. *Answers to Tough Questions Skeptics Ask About the Christian Faith.* Wheaton, IL: Tyndale House Publishers, Inc., 1980.

Yancey, Philip. *The Jesus I Never Knew.* Grand Rapids, MI: Zondervan Publishing House, 1995.

Organizations and Web Sites

Christian Science—Former Members
Ananias (Pilgrims to the Cross of Christ from Christian Science)
  Web site: www.ananias.org
CHILD (Children's Healthcare is a Legal Duty, Inc.)
  136 Blue Heron Place
  Lexington, KY 40511
  E-mail: admin@childrenshealthcare.org
  Web site: www.childrenshealthcare.org
Christian Way (Former Christian Scientists for Jesus Christ)
  Box 39607
  Phoenix, AZ 85069
  Phone: (602) 973-4768
  Fax: (602) 789-7165
  E-mail: cw@christianway.org
  Web site: www.christianway.org

Counter-cult (secular)
ICSA (International Cultic Studies Association)
  Box 2265
  Bonita Springs, FL 34133
  Phone: (239) 514-3081
  Fax: (305) 393-8193
  E-mail: mail@icsamail.com
  Web site: www.icsahome.com

Counter-cult (Christian)
Watchman Fellowship, Inc.
  913 Huffman Road
  Birmingham, AL 35215
  Phone: (205) 833-2858
  Fax: (205) 833-8699
  Web site: www.watchman.org

Counseling Services

Wellspring Retreat and Resource Center
    525 Richland Ave.
    Athens, OH 45701
    Web site: www.wellspringretreat.org

Made in the USA
Monee, IL
04 January 2022

87911954R00115